You Can Play...

TENNIS

IN 2 HOURS

You Can Play...
TENNIS
IN 2 HOURS

OSCAR WEGNER

Foreword by Bud Collins

Publishers Since 1798

THOMAS NELSON PUBLISHERS
NASHVILLE

Grateful acknowledgment is made here to Carlos Alves, of Florianopolis, Brazil, for research facilities.

Photography location courtesy of The Racquet Club of Boca Raton, Boca Raton, Florida.

Picture of the "Swing Master" (Registered Trademark), used with permission of Pedro Mena, 3706 Woods Walk Blvd., Lake Worth, Florida 33467.

Cover photo by Suzanna Collins. Photos on pages 23, 25, 27, 30, 32, 34, 36, 38, 39, 40, 41, 42, 43, 46, 49, 51, 52, 54, 56, and 57 by Russ Adams Productions.

Published in Nashville, Tennessee, by Thomas Nelson, Inc., Publishers and distributed in Canada by Lawson Falle, Ltd., Cambridge, Ontario.

Library of Congress Cataloging-in-Publication Data

Wegner, Oscar.
    Tennis in two hours : the techniques that make tennis an easy sport to learn / by Oscar Wegner.
       p.   cm.
   ISBN 0-8407-6806-0
   1. Tennis. I. Title. II. Tennis in 2 hours.
GV995.W44   1992
796.342—dc20
                                             91–37389
                                             CIP

1 2 3 4 5 — 96 95 94 93 92

Dedication

To the United States of America.

It is not by accident that I wrote this book in English and published it in the United States.

America's wonderful people and their hospitality have made my life very pleasant in many ways.

In exchange, I want to help America reconquer its former tennis glory, and my hope is that this book will help achieve that goal.

<u>You can write to the author</u>

The author welcomes any questions, enquiries or commentary. Please include a self-addressed stamped envelope when you write to: Oscar Wegner, P.O. Box 810384, Boca Raton, Florida, 33481.

Acknowledgments

To all my friends, students and fellow pros, who were an inspiration and driving force for me, and especially, Steve Schulman for encouraging me to write this book, Marsha May for teaching me to write in English, Pedro Mena for photographs, David Bishop for computer technical support, and Karen Sylvester, Martin Mulligan, Jurgen Fassbender, Art and Ellen Mills, Jimmy Sternberg, Steve Weicholz, Carlos Alves, Marcos Reblin, David and Mary Ziff, Jana Hunsaker, Sheri Slobin, David Glackin, Scott Leatherman; my friends at the Creek Club in Locust Valley, Alan Quasha, Roberto Mendoza, Kristina Sywolsky, Jeff Phipps and many more; and my friends and associates at Thomas Nelson Publishers, my greatest appreciation and gratitude.

Student Guide

Advanced players:

Read through Chapter 3, then go to the specific stroke or area of your game which you want to improve.

Beginners:

1 Read "Introduction."
2 Read "How to Read this Book." From here on read only the *italic* type.
2b If you need help choosing a racket, go to page 231.
3 Read "Caution" (page 13).
4 Read Chapter 4 "Basics and Definitions."
5 Read Chapter 5 "Checking and Developing your Coordination," doing drills #1 through #6.
6 Read Chapter 6 "Grip and Racket Position," doing drills #1, #2 and #3.
7 Read Chapter 7 "The Forehand," doing drills #1 through #10.
8 Read page 115 in Chapter 8. If you choose to learn the backhand stroke two-handed, continue reading Chapter 8 and do drills #1 through #10. If you choose to learn the backhand stroke one-handed, skip Chapter 8 and go directly to Chapter 9 (page 123). Read this chapter, doing drills #1 through #7.
9 Read Chapter 10 "The Serve," doing drills #1 through #7.
10 Read Chapter 11 "The Rally Game." Find a nice partner and play as directed until you are satisfied with your game.
11 Invite any good player to play with you (without them slamming the ball). Enjoy your game and the rest of this book.

Contents

Foreword

I know people who couldn't learn tennis in two lifetimes—but they never met Oscar Wegner.

As Oscar's encore, will he write "Nuclear Physics Over the Weekend"? Or "How to Breed and Ride a Kentucky Derby Winner on Your Lunch Hours"?

I'm waiting.

Unfortunately for you nuclear physics and Kentucky Derby fans, Oscar Wegner is a one-track guy. But fortunately for you who have a better idea—that tennis is a wonderful game to learn and play—Oscar's track isn't Churchill Downs. Instead it's a short course in tennis to a photo finish. A photo of you playing tennis, hitting balls over the net. Lots of them. Soon.

As Bjorn Borg used to say, "It's a simple game. Just hit the ball over the net one more time than your opponent." That's the essence, all right. And, with Oscar, it can be fairly simple. In fact, I think of Oscar Wegner as "Dr. Simplicity" in getting the essentials across to players of all levels. Especially those who have no level at all—but want to find one.

As I consider Oscar's methods, I'm reminded of this line from an avid hacker, the actor-comedian Alan King: "I've got a ten-thousand-dollar forehand—and a ten cent backhand." King was drolly referring to all the money he'd spent on lessons, and he was still only halfway there.

But I don't know of any player, Boris Becker or Monica Seles,

John McEnroe or Martina Navratilova—even that wily senior citizen, James Scott Connors—who feels all the way there. And they're the gifted ones. Yet they know that improvement is still just a few swings away.

And the improvement you're looking for, I think, is from zero (or near-zero) to respectability and playing comfort. Dr. Simplicity can supply it in most cases because of his think-less, natural approach. Wegner's Way, I feel, would have amazed Alan King and so many others who've devoted so much time to taking lessons.

Wegner strips instruction of all those accepted phrases and directions that usually only clutter your mind and confuse. I saw it in person during the two days Oscar worked with four of my own kids (ranging from 16 to 30) plus a 7-year-old granddaughter. She, the youngest, was brand-new to the game. Two of the rest had played some; the other two had hardly touched a racket previously. All were hitting the ball back and forth before long, and keeping it going. Definitely progressing. What struck me so pleasantly was that their desire to play had been refreshed or freshly kindled.

Naturally it's great to have Oscar himself on court with you, but, failing that, I'm confident this book—Oscar in print—will be a splendid foundation to start you off or moving ahead.

Where was Oscar when so many people needed him? He was out there, playing the circuit, learning, teaching and refining as his streamlined fun-through-simplicity methods took shape.

I met this congenial Argentine in 1973 at Miami Beach where he was coaching the Spanish Junior boys team in the worldwide Sunshine Cup tournament. Those kids were hitting extra hard and with plenty of topspin in a way that startled spectators—and me.

Such shotmaking would soon electrify the pro tour as delivered by the nimble Swede, Bjorn Borg, and the burly Argentine, Guillermo Vilas. Eventually both of them were elevated to the International Tennis Hall of Fame at Newport, R.I.

Tennis really began to cook in the American public eye with the inspirational arrival of Borg and Vilas as well as Chris Evert and Jimmy Connors in the early 70s. Also, there were a couple of landmark events on TV instrumental in launching the tennis boom (epidemic?) in the U.S.

In 1972, those diminutive Australian strokemaking geniuses, Rod Laver and Ken Rosewall, enthralled a NBC audience for 3½ hours in a magnificent 5-set battle for the World Championship Tennis title in Dallas. Somehow Rosewall overcame Laver by merely two points, 7-5 in the fifth set tie-breaker. No closer final—and, perhaps, no better one—has ever been played. That match had people talking tennis enthusiastically.

Sixteen months later, September of 1973, there was Billie Jean and Bobby's babbling Battle of the Sexes in Houston's Astrodome. Who cared if it was a schlock-'round-the-clock promotion? A record tennis crowd of more than 30,000 and sky-high ratings on ABC showed that viewers were captivated by the geezer and the gal: 56-year-old ex-Wimbledon champ Bobby Riggs in mixed singles against 29-year-old Billie Jean King, evangelist of the women's tour. Interest was so phenomenal that bookmakers handled the action.

Swinging her racket like Joan of Arc's battle-ax, Billie Jean achieved a poetically just result in straight sets, and everybody wanted to play tennis.

Racket and clothing sales soared. So did ticket sales and tournament acquisitions by TV networks. Tennis courts, indoor and out, sprouted. But was this growth spurt merely a fad? Yes and no. Despite a fall-off, tennis did make substantial gains in interest and participation that held.

But there was a fundamental problem even though tennis looked and felt terrific to play. Terrific, that is, if you could play. But it wasn't all that easy to learn. And it took a frustrating while. Many learners were quickly discouraged, and gave up.

The outstanding need was for uncomplicated basic training—instruction utilizing natural instincts, and quick to grasp. Enter Dr. Simplicity.

Oscar may also be "Dr. Contradictory" for those of you who've had earlier instruction because he asks you to empty your mind of any previous teaching. But I think you'll find it worthwhile to dump the past and join Oscar in your tennis future. In listening to him I've unlearned a few things myself that I long considered gospel.

With Oscar I'm convinced you'll learn simply and simply have fun. You may not embark on a career with the pros, but to me the main thing is to play and enjoy—to be a respectable hacker. There are a lot more of us hackers than there are wage-winning pros, and we have a lot more fun than they do.

Remember, blessed be the hackers, for we shall inherit the mirth. Meanwhile, good luck in following Wegner's Way to making a solid hit.

Bud Collins
Boston Globe/NBC

Introduction

Ever wonder why top tennis pros like Bjorn Borg, Ivan Lendl, Mats Wilander, Andre Agassi, Boris Becker and Steffi Graf hit such great forehands in an open stance,* while your pro drills you to put your left foot forward and close** your stance?

Why those tennis greats wait until the last possible moment to take the racket back, while you are constantly drilled to take your racket back as soon as you see the ball coming your way?

Why they bend the arm in the follow-through while your pro teaches you to keep your arm straight?

Ever wonder why John McEnroe, Ivan Lendl, Jimmy Connors, Chris Evert, Martina Navratilova, and just about everyone else in the pro ranks turn and run straight to the ball, while you are taught to sidestep first and then turn before you hit?

*Open stance: Feet facing the net.
**Closed stance: Feet facing the sideline.

These pros play a totally different game of tennis than what is taught by conventional teaching techniques, but it's obviously the right way to play the game.

And it's a game that you can—and should—be playing yourself.

By reading this book and following the techniques taught here, you can learn true championship tennis the way the top pros play the game.

The reason that these pros are so good is not that they are superhuman. They just concentrate on very simple things, like waiting for the ball, finding it and guiding it with their racket. They do these things instinctively, and many times they don't understand why people have trouble with simple shots.

There are a myriad of misconceptions about tennis, and they all make a simple sport very difficult. Most tennis teaching systems introduce you to many details and mental images of body positions that a typical player finds difficult to coordinate. You may have perfect positioning and a perfect stroke, but the ball may be going somewhere other than where you want, or, depending on your advancement, you may miss hitting it at all.

If you are an advanced player or a pro, you'll be reading the "Misconceptions" chapter shortly after this introduction. You'll have an idea of how the wrong concepts can affect your improvement or block your way to the top.

If you are a beginner, you can use this book to train yourself to play a winning game simply by using the unique techniques and drills I have developed in years of teaching the game . . . the techniques I reveal in a special section for beginners.

By using this book you can learn tennis in a very simple way, just like the top pros play. This book is set up so that with each chapter you can go on the court and do the drills to learn each particular stroke. The section on "How to Read This Book" explains the learning procedure.

This book is different from the conventional way of teaching tennis. It is not change for the sake of change. This technology works fast and produces the desired results.

My teaching techniques emphasize the development of a strong feel and control of the ball. Almost everyone strives for control of one kind or another in the physical universe. When you learn to drive a car, for example, you like to keep it on the road and away from trees and ditches. It doesn't help to have someone at your side telling you things that make you think too much. You want to know only the important things. Then, without anyone nagging you, you want to get a *feel* for it, you want to do some easy driving.

When you learn to play tennis, you'd like to keep the ball in play and in the court. The less you have to remember, the easier it will be for you to get a *feel* for it. That is exactly how the top pros play, thinking as little as possible. They focus on the feel of the ball with a simple, uncomplicated technique which they found to work at some time in their career.

And yes, you can learn to play tennis quickly. It is an easy sport to learn—but only if you know the correct technique.

Most of the absolute beginners I teach can play with me from the backcourt in less than ninety minutes. By then they keep the ball in play, back and forth, twenty to thirty times, or more. Learning to serve with the techniques described in this book takes another twenty to thirty minutes. In two hours they are ready for a game, playing comfortably back and forth.

Students who learn from the beginning with these methods, without interference from harmful techniques, develop their game to high standards over the years. I tested this in a small city in Brazil, Florianopolis, capital of the state of Santa Catarina. In 1982 I taught this system to several teaching pros. By 1985 some of their juniors were winning national championships. The teaching techniques started to spread through the state. By 1988 they ranked third in Brazil in junior tennis and had several top national juniors, some internationally ranked. By then they had surpassed large states like Rio de Janeiro, and they are now in a close race with Rio Grande do Sul (Porto Alegre) for second place.

Experienced Players

This book is not only for the beginner but for the advanced player as well. In most chapters I expose misconceptions that are deeply entrenched in this sport.

If you already play, at any level, but you have trouble improving and feeling the ball in any of your shots, it will help you to take a fresh look at the basics described here. More often than not, trouble with the basics is all it takes for a problem with a stroke to exist. By straightening out the basics, you'll see improvement right away.

I organized this book so that beginners can find their way through without being overwhelmed or confused. The advanced player, on the other hand, should read the early chapters and then look up the subject of interest, according to the personal level of advancement or the area to be improved. Chapter Three, "How to Correct Faulty Strokes" shows how to apply the data in this book to make improvements on a stroke.

For the advanced player, the new technical data may rearrange what the player has absorbed through the years. Many times this older information is what the player had to adopt to survive on the court. Much of it may be compensations the player developed to make up for weaknesses and faults, perhaps viewed through some faulty concepts that now stand in the way of any further improvement. In view of the new technical data taught here, players can change viewpoints and judge the older data from a new angle. One can then understand past failures and successes. It will reinforce the positive things, as well as clarifying why something went wrong, and what is risky and what is not.

The Starting Partner

If you are going on the court for the first time, you'll need another person to learn with. Usually the best partner is someone who will be striving for control and long rallies.*

Many players would rather "kill" the ball, like banging on a piano, instead of playing it as nicely as they can. They are no help to you. If necessary, trade that hard-playing, macho player for someone who will toss you the ball nicely with their hand, whether they play tennis or not.

To learn each step you need a slow-paced ball, not far from your reach. When you are ready, you and your friend can slowly step up the pace without losing control.

It might be helpful to have your partner read the first chapters of this book, including the area you are developing at the time, in order to understand what you are trying to accomplish.

If you are being helped by an experienced player, have him or her read Chapter Two on "Misconceptions" before they go on the court with you. Most "experts" give many gratuitous tips without knowing that most are barriers to the learning process.

You can also do some learning on your own. Go out on the court and practice some of the techniques in this book, while tossing the ball within your reach. See how the ball behaves, what you feel and what you accomplish. Some of the drills can be done against a wall. Just be careful not to groove-in the incorrect technique.

The techniques in this book are not the only ones you can use, but they are the most efficient both for teaching and for playing. This style is the foundation of the game most top tennis professionals play today.

*Rally: The ball going back and forth.

Why This Book Was Written

For advanced players only. Beginners should go directly to the next section, "How to Read this Book," on page 11.

What separates this teaching system from the rest? What makes it better? Why was it necessary to create it? What is wrong with conventional teaching techniques?

The techniques taught in this book are amazingly effective because they are extremely simple. They don't try to override things that you learned at a very tender age. You focus only on what you are doing with your hand and the ball, while the rest is coordinated in an instinctive way you probably learned before you were five years old.

Conventional teaching techniques, on the contrary, draw your attention to many distractions. They point to the position of your feet, body, weight balance. They give you mental images to follow which may differ drastically from the hand-eye coordination you learned as a child.

For instance, the part most often tampered with is the backswing, the part of the swing prior to contact with the ball. Most tennis teachers consider it a separate part of the swing and something you must control consciously. But look at the top professionals. You'll see that they all have different ways of taking the racket back. The backswing is their own personal way of "finding" the ball, while generating power at the same time. This is a very delicate thing that they developed themselves and shouldn't be disturbed. New players can be directed to develop their own backswing, in a path that uses the exact imprints of early life experiences.

This is what this book is all about—integration of technique with your past.

Every one of us has had different experiences in life, including how we learned hand-eye coordination. When you want to learn tennis, that is the equipment you have to play with, something that is uniquely yours.

One way to wreck it is to show the student the arm motion prior to the forward swing. Learning with your teacher's mental pictures won't help you either—it will probably hinder you.

You learn where your right foot goes, and your left foot, to keep your racket head up in a perfect loop, with your little derriere nicely sticking out. But then, when you coordinate these things perfectly and you see the ball mysteriously flying by your racket without making contact, or not going where you want, you'll wonder what kind of game this is. Is something wrong with your coordination or should you just forget it and go home?

Well, this is what *conventional* tennis teaching has done to many—driven them home.

Back in the 1960s we had close to ten million tennis players in the U.S. A big boom began in the late 1960s with the advent of Open Tennis* and big TV exposure. By the late 1970s, according to industry figures, over thirty million Americans were playing tennis.

In the 1980s this figure was way down, close to twenty million. How did we manage to lose ten million players?

The answer is easy: discouragement. The belief at that time was, and still is, that tennis is a difficult sport.

And that is partly true. Because *it was made* a difficult sport, especially in this country, where the hunger for technology is so high,

---

*Open Tennis: Major championships open to amateurs and professionals alike.

and where people seek and pay for instruction in anything they want to do. The misconceptions about tennis are so common that it takes a superhuman or a very lucky person to make it through this maze of misinformation.

Purpose

The purpose of this book is to clean up the misconceptions about this wonderful, exciting sport, and to teach a natural, new way of learning tennis. This book may be a rude awakening for many wonderful people involved in the tennis teaching profession. It is meant to be my contribution to your success.

How to Read This Book

How you read this book depends on your tennis experience.

If you are in the beginning stages or you have never played tennis, go directly to Chapter Four, "Basics and Definitions," where the italic type begins.

Up to Chapter Twelve you only need to read the *italic type to learn to play. The rest of the data is technical information that clarifies and reinforces these techniques for the more experienced player.*

As a matter of fact, you can go out onto the court with the book, read a section on a drill, and do it. Then read the next drill and do that one. Then the next, and so on, until you finish the series of drills in that particular chapter. Now you are ready for the next chapter.

The text printed in italic is all you need to read to become an accomplished backcourt player. That is the intent of this book. The first half of the book is geared to making you proficient in the most important facet of this sport—the backcourt game. The net game* is explained after that, and then the special shots, but they are intended for much later in your development.

There are chapters toward the end of this book that explain tennis racket size, weight, grip, and also the rules of the game and types of courts. If you have any questions as to what racket to use, or any other technical detail, you can read those at any time.

You may skip the rest of this section after the italic type ends, except for the CAUTION note at the end, also in italic type. Then go

*Net game: Playing close to the net.

directly to Chapter Four, "Basics and Definitions," and then to Chapter Five, where the coordination drills start. Do the drills and then go to Chapter Six for your basic grip and racket position.

Now you are ready for Chapter Seven, "The Forehand." Do the drills described there one by one, reading just the italic type. When you finish the drills described in Chapter Seven, you'll know close to fifty percent of the backcourt game. You are then ready for the following chapters.

By the end of Chapter Eleven you could probably rally with anyone at a slow or medium pace.

Whenever you are tired, rest. Learning several chapters should not be done in one day, unless you are a highly trained athlete. Stamina and strength vary so much that you need to be the judge as to when your session should end.

Even the drills in one chapter may be too strenuous to be done in one session, especially in the heat of a summer day. Don't overdo it. Continue the next day or the next weekend.

The Learning Process

As you progress you'll be able to handle more and more difficulty. Learning is a process on a gradient. If the degree of difficulty is too steep, you may get confused. If this happens, I recommend that you go back to the fundamentals until you regain your feeling for the ball and your confidence.

I describe the materials in this book as twofold: drills and technical data. We can refer to the drills as the action and to the technical data as thought. In order for you to learn to do anything properly, you need to have a balance between action and thought.

Because tennis is a game of feel and action in the physical universe rather than inside your mind, this balance needs to be heavily weighted toward the physical. Just reading the drill to be done next will give you enough of the necessary concepts. You then do the drill long enough to feel you've got it. Then go to the next drill, and so on. When you finish the drills in a chapter, you'll have that particular aspect of the game under your control.

If you then want to take a rest and get more information, sit down and read the technical explanation in regular type, but only in the chapters in which you did all the drills. You are now an "experienced" player, but only up to the point that you have practiced.

Experienced Players

The process is different for the experienced player who has already hit thousands of balls. You have enough active training under your belt to be able to take in a lot of technical data without being overwhelmed. An accomplished player could read this entire book without interruption and be able to recall examples from experience and from things seen.

However, even an experienced player might be in for a surprise. In each chapter there are new concepts or new approaches that can reshape or modify an intimate part of an advanced player's game.

CAUTION

This book has been designed so that you learn step by step. You need to feel comfortable about each step before going on to the next. If you feel that you have made too big a jump and that you are losing your control, check to see if you are putting too much difficulty into the drill. For example, your friend may be tossing the ball too fast for you or too far from you. If you have adjusted this and still don't feel comfortable, go back to the previous drills to see if you missed something. If you are confused, check to see if there is a concept or a word in this book that you didn't understand and clear it up. Any of these things can distract your attention and affect your performance.

NOTE

The methods in this book can be used by anyone to teach a child or an adult, whether you play tennis or not.

Very young children need much more time to develop their strokes, because the muscle development is still in process.

Teach slowly, be patient and understanding. Teach for short periods of time. Consult the students regarding their understanding of the lesson and their willingness to continue.

Treat your students as you would like to be treated yourself.

1

Modern Tennis and Topspin

In the last two decades professional tennis has taken a big jump technically with the acceptance and use of topspin among most players.

Topspin is a forward roll, just as if the ball were rolling forward on the ground. It is created by brushing up on the ball while stroking. You lift the racket much higher than the intended line of flight of the ball.

A BIT OF TOPSPIN

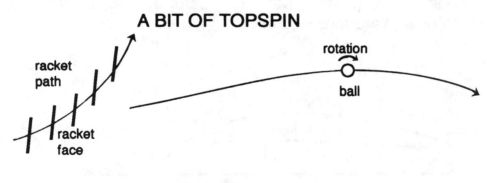

A LOT OF TOPSPIN

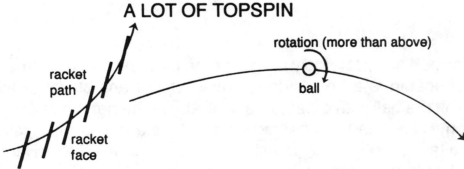

The air friction on top of the ball will be considerably higher than that on the bottom. The air below the ball will escape much faster, creating a zone of lower air pressure that will also slow the ball and pull it down.

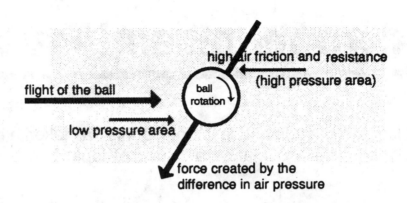

That, in addition to the force of gravity, makes for a much more pronounced downward curve. The ball will drop much sooner than if it had no spin at all (a "flat" ball). The faster the ball rotates forward, the more downward force it gets.

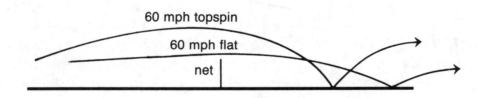

Although still not widely taught at the beginner and intermediate levels, topspin is a tremendous advantage to any player. It allows you to hit the ball with great force, well above the net, knowing that it will come down in the opponent's court. The ball is also going to take quite a jump, making it difficult for your opponent to advance to the net or to hit a winner from the backcourt.

This happens very often at the professional level. You see many rallies between the top players in the world where the ball doesn't clear the service line by much, but it is still very effective in keeping the other player back.

High Topspin

A ball hit high with a lot of topspin slows down as it goes forward and up. Then it accelerates as it comes down, making it difficult to judge how the ball will bounce. Such a ball usually kicks high and toward the backcourt. That makes high topspin effective, even on hard courts, in keeping your opponent back.

Confidence Builder

Topspin is a great tool and also a confidence builder. When you are afraid of missing you don't have to hit a softer shot to be safe. You know the ball is going to drop in the court if you rotate it enough. Your fear doesn't show since you don't need to slow down play to keep the ball in the court.

With topspin, you can also clear the net by a wider margin. With practice you get the feel that the more you hit up, the more the ball comes down. That is why I teach this technique to the beginner, the intermediate, the advanced player, and the pros who haven't mastered it yet. It encourages them to hit much harder, even under pressure.

When to Learn Topspin

The techniques used in this book to teach groundstrokes develop topspin naturally, right from the beginning.

Although this learning is done at slow speeds at first, the swing developed is the same low-to-high stroke used by the pros.

I consider this a very basic part of learning to play tennis well. Topspin requires that you apply much more upward force to the ball than the intended path of your shot.

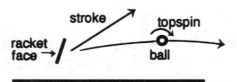

If, on the contrary, you learn from the beginning to apply your force coincident with the intended line of flight of your shot, it will become an instinctive habit, something that will be difficult to shake in the future. You hit the ball with a certain direction of effort and you relate this action to the speed and height of your shot, and to where the ball lands. If I later tell you to lift your strokes with topspin, you'll probably panic. You'll be afraid of hitting the ball too high and too far.

You may understand it intellectually, but deep inside you are conditioned differently from your prior experience. You haven't instinctively built the feel that comes with topspin: the more you hit up on the ball and the more you roll it, the more it comes down.

Players who have hit flat most of their lives and now want to hit topspin, may need hundreds of hours of practice to master this new feel.

For all these reasons I like to see beginners hit up and use topspin to bring the ball down in the court, rather than forcing the ball down as soon as they develop some faster shots. Their tennis instinct is virgin territory. A beginner needs to get the feeling from the start that lifting the stroke causes the ball to curve down.

Not one of the beginners I taught with topspin was afraid of hitting the ball out. Whenever their shots went beyond the baseline, they rolled the next ball more.

Topspin builds up your confidence. Flat hits cause innumerable errors, lessening your confidence.

As you progress as a topspin player, you'll learn to rotate the ball more and more efficiently, whether on your forehand, backhand, or serve. The safety factor in your shots will always be in your favor. Should you decide to risk a few, you can hit some flatter shots, but you can always revert to safety when needed by going back to top-spin strokes.

You also need to get used to seeing topspin balls coming at you. Because of the rotation, topspin balls jump on the bounce, making them more difficult to handle. Getting used to it as a natural thing, right from the beginning, will make anyone a much better player.

2

Misconceptions

CAUTION: This chapter may "spin" even a very serious tennis player, shaking data that perhaps took years to instill. Recommended dosage: One item at a time until fully digested.

Why is tennis considered a difficult sport to learn? Mostly because of widely taught misconceptions that cripple a player's natural ability and make coordination as difficult as if you were walking with several crutches at the same time.

Even many tennis professionals believe these misconceptions. But the test is, do they actually follow them when they play?

Observe and decide for yourself.

I have seen great players go into rapid decline in the later years of their career when adjusting to the conventional way.

During their greatest years, of course, they were untouchable. Nobody could tell them to use any other technique but their own obviously successful style.

But soon after they felt some cracks in their armor they sought advice. "Flatten your strokes. You are getting older, you need more power," is one of the culprits.

For many great modern players—Rod Laver, Bjorn Borg, Ivan Lendl, Boris Becker, Guillermo Vilas, Martina Navratilova (forehand) and Chris Evert (backhand)—the topspin strokes were a great rung on their ladder to success. At the top of their game, they could hit as hard as they wanted, sometimes flattening their strokes. But when their confidence waned, perhaps during a slump, the successful course of action was to rely on the safety of the topspin shots, without compromising the power or the margin for error.

John McEnroe flattened his groundstrokes after a lengthy layoff. His game deteriorated. Fortunately for him, and for American tennis, he went back to his artistry and to his topspin lift and made it back up the ranks.

Common Tennis Misconceptions

> *MYTH:* **You have to learn every move—tennis is a game of positions, of peculiar steps and preparations that you have to learn in detail.**
>
> *FACT:* **Top pros get to the ball in a natural, instinctive way, focusing only on what they do with the racket and the ball.**

Tennis is a flowing game, a game of togetherness with the ball. While the ball is in play, you think of nothing—observing, running, "feeling," and controlling the ball. Your racket is an extension of your hand. The rest of your body accompanies the hand naturally, without worrying about coordination or footwork.

You probably learned to move like that years ago, when you learned to walk, to run, to catch something falling or thrown at you.

Nobody needs to tell you now that your right foot takes one step, then your left foot takes one step, and so on. Nobody should even make you think of that, changing your focus from controlling the ball, or dividing it with things that you would do naturally anyway.

In the mind of a tennis pro a groundstroke is a channeled effort rather than thought. His eyes are focused on the ball, his "feel" is focused on what he does with the racket, as its movement and angle determine his whole shot. He wants to feel the ball, rather than think of the mechanics.

Boris Becker

The player gets to the proximity of the ball, "finding" it as if wanting to catch it. He now thinks of nothing else but where he wants to send the ball, channeling all his effort to get the ball there. In his mind the only mental image picture of "position" is of the arm at the end of the swing, something he has related to his shot placement over the years.

His mental effort may be nothing more than to get the arm and racket to this "finish." When he gets the arm there this particular effort is done, and he might keep the arm in this position for a short time, "feeling" the end of his swing and looking to see where the ball is going.

His legs don't stay still. He may already be recovering from the shot or covering the court. But he has certainly related the end of his swing to where his shot has landed.

Most conventional teaching techniques make you relate the impact with the ball to your shot's placement. That is excellent for your volleys. But on their groundstrokes, top pros think of the finish of the swing.

That is the main reason why the great players don't "choke," stopping their swing midway. The only part of the swing they know for sure is this "finish." The rest of the stroke adjusts instinctively while finding the ball.

MYTH: **You have to react as fast as you can.**

FACT: **Top professionals restrain themselves from reacting too quickly.**

Although sometimes there is little time to get ready, you have to manage time depending on how much time you have. With the ball at a medium or slow pace, a pro looks as if he isn't even trying.

So low is the effort required at this slower pace that many amateurs play great placement and control games seemingly without exerting themselves. They take their time to run and to stroke. They look terrifically coordinated. They don't look like pros, of course, because the speed of the ball is much slower. But they play like pros, managing time and effort efficiently.

Just look at a pro warming up or practicing and you'll see how easily he moves and how much time he's got.

Ivan Lendl

At high ball speeds it may look different, but there isn't much upper body effort on the groundstrokes prior to the hit. A pro finds the ball first, then explodes.

Of course, your legs have to move fast to get you to the ball. A good opponent will make you run, slide, bend, jump. But while the legs go fast, the arms are waiting for the right time to swing.

What is amazing about the top pros is the separation between the body effort to get to the ball and the arm effort to strike it. They run for the ball first, trying to find it as if catching it, then they swing at it.

Conventional tennis teaching emphasizes taking the racket back as soon as you see the ball coming your way. The student does this preparation before starting to run, losing valuable time that should be used to get to the ball. Even at high ball speeds, this preparation should be done towards the end of the run.

MYTH: **Take your racket back as soon as the ball leaves your opponent's racket.**

FACT: **The best pro players keep the racket to their front until the ball is close.**

Keeping the racket to the front keeps the racket closer to the ball and helps find it really well. Although pros turn their shoulders, that is different from taking the arm back. Many top pros keep the non-playing hand on the racket during the first part of the flight of the ball to avoid taking the racket back too soon. The ball bounces first, gets close to the player, then he swings at it.

Taking the racket back early is probably the most common barrier to advancement taught in tennis today.

The racket is already in the forehand-ready position when holding it centered at your waist. The same accounts for the two-handed backhand, where grip changes are unnecessary.

Only if you have a one-handed backhand and you see the ball coming to your left side do you need to change your grip together with your turn to the left to get to the ball. You need to pull the racket head back, while your right hand goes forward and away from your body. This changes the grip automatically. You are ready! Many players accomplish the same by pointing the racket butt to the incoming ball.

Steffi Graf

Modern forehands and two-handed backhands are totally different from the old racket-back technique. Instead of taking the racket back right away, you "stalk" the ball with the racket face, as if you were going to touch it. Then you hit. This "stalking" helps find the ball well. It also adjusts the backswing automatically to the speed and height of the ball, and to the difficulty of the shot.

Although a top player's swing may look the same over and over, it has adjustments for every ball.

You may approach the path of the ball from the moment it leaves your opponent's racket. You may start to adjust your arms. But beware of committing your swing.

Taking your backswing early commits you to a swing path *before* you know exactly where the ball will be, which occurs *after* the bounce.

Predicting exactly how the ball will bounce is not possible. Court surfaces are uneven in texture and the ball may grab the ground differently depending on its speed and spin. With these variables, the best you'll have is an approximation.

If you start your groundstroke as soon as possible, prior to the bounce, you may have a perfect stroke in theory. But it will be one that will have to be adjusted to the bounce of the ball halfway through.

This is the way most people played tennis throughout much of the history of the sport. They started their swing and then they adjusted as they were going through the ball.

Only a few players excelled in hitting their groundstrokes from the ball forward, rather than behind it, and they became the best players of their time.

In modern professional tennis, this technique has been widely accepted, especially by European and South American players.

At the high speeds of professional play sometimes there doesn't seem to be enough time. But there is!

Most pro players don't consciously know that they wait, but they do. It is an inner mechanism that they developed in the early stages of their game.

If you asked a world class player, "In mixed doubles, would you take more time to return Chris Evert's first serve than McEnroe's?" the answer would be, "Of course I would." This shows that deep inside, the player waits for the right moment to stroke.

Here is a simple experiment that may convince some staunch supporters of the *racket-back-early* technique that they should change their approach.

Get another player to serve to your forehand. Take your racket back before he starts his service motion, and keep it there while he gets ready to serve. When he serves, return from this backswing arm position.

See how awkward it feels? I have done this experiment with some very good players and it stiffened their returns. I was also told it felt awful.

If you have ever wondered why so many beginners have trouble learning with the conventional *racket back* system, this is your answer.

Good coordination means doing things at the proper time. In your groundstrokes, learn to play the second curve of the ball, that is, the curve after the bounce.

Try this in practice. Start with slow, high-looping groundstrokes. Choose your contact point before you take your racket back for momentum. That contact point becomes apparent only after the bounce. On slow, high-looping balls, it occurs *well after the bounce*.

Can you picture that you have to wait as much as possible before taking your racket back? I know that this will be mentally difficult to those who have trained for years by the opposite method. You'll feel so late!

Starting your swing too early is a hard habit to break. But the player who waits for the right moment to swing will thrive. He'll find the ball so well—he'll feel it so much—hitting either softly or at tremendous speeds. Ask McEnroe what it feels like. He is a master at it, just as Nastase was some years ago.

Both players had an incredible combination of feel, ball speed, and touch. They adjusted their timing perfectly to the arrival of the ball.

You can do the same, provided you learn to wait for the ball.

Andre Agassi

MYTH: **Hit the ball early.**

FACT: **You have to wait for the ball.**

Hitting the ball early is a concept that needs to be clarified, even at the highest level of the game. I have seen too many pros have off days and not know exactly why.

It is one thing to advance on the court to cut your opponent's time, or to hit on the rise, putting pressure on your opponent, but it is another thing to start the stroke earlier than needed.

Of course top players like to attack the ball, hitting it firmly; but at high ball speeds, a couple of hundredths of a second too early, and the magic is gone. Errors keep creeping up, and the player doesn't understand what is happening. The "feel" is off.

For players who lift the ball with topspin, being slightly early makes it harder to lift. If facing a player with heavy topspin, being too early makes for many mis-hits.

At the top pro level, perhaps it is not noticed as a mis-hit, but the response is weaker, less lively, sometimes shorter.

The tennis ball is very lively. If you wait perfectly, approach the ball slowly with the racket and accelerate from contact with the ball on, you'll feel that the ball stays on your strings longer, then takes off.

Your eyes cannot grasp all that, but if you hit a few balls this way you'll feel the difference. It is definitely a different feel—more solid, longer, more control. You won't get those sudden spurts of ball speed where you don't know what made the ball go so fast even when you were restraining your swing.

The ball speed, even when applying the same amount of force, depends on how close to the contact point you start to apply your force. A bit too early, and you get plenty of power, but your control is gone.

If a pro persists in hitting earlier than usual, perhaps unaware that he is just a few hundredths of a second sooner that day, or that this particular court plays a shade slower than the one he practiced on, he starts losing his confidence. He starts tightening up. His feel is lessened, his touch is gone, and deep inside he is puzzled— *why?*

This is more likely to happen to players who relish earlier timing to get more ball speed. They are playing with fire, very close to the boundary of being too early. But on better days, the magic, the brilliance, are there. They just seem to touch the ball and it shoots like lightning, streaking to the opponent's court.

The heavy topspin players, on the other hand, wait for the ball so much that it hurts. They have to muscle the ball much more than the earlier hitters to get the same ball speed, but for timing they are in a safer zone. The chances of hitting too early are minimal. They would have to be off close to a tenth of a second, a fact more easily noticeable than the hundredths of a second that would throw off the earlier hitter.

If you feel that this is hard to grasp, go out on the court. Toss the ball a little in front and to your side. Wait till after the bounce, with almost no backswing. Feel that you touch the ball before you hit it,

Monica Seles

then emphasize your follow-through. In the first few shots the ball may be going nowhere at all, but as you hit harder you'll gradually get to know how close to the ball you have to start accelerating to get both ball speed and maximum control.

You can observe that most of the pros play this way. Most errors in pro tennis come from taking the arm back too soon or stroking too soon. You lose feel, you lose control.

Chris Evert, for example, used to be much earlier on her forehand than on her backhand. Most of her errors came from her forehand side. Her backhand was her most terrifying shot, not only for its accuracy, but also for its topspin.

In the last few years of her career she learned to wait longer on her forehand, making it a very reliable stroke. On the backhand side she chose to hit the ball earlier, flatter and well in front to get more power. Most of her errors came from her backhand side, in some matches totaling more unforced errors with this shot than with all strokes combined when she was at her peak.

This does not mean that you can't hit some balls early, or well in front, thus flattening your stroke. You just have to consider the risk factor involved. You may hit some great winners, but it may also cost you points. The real risk is not on the power, but in losing the topspin on the ball.

This topspin, even if minimal, helps to drop the ball into the court. One or two ball rotations difference between your hit and the landing of your shot at higher speeds, may mean the difference of a foot or two in the length of your shot. The ball that used to drop just inside the line may go out.

Repeated errors like that will erode a player's confidence, precipitating his or her decline.

It is better to strike further back within the correct striking zone—getting more topspin and control, still with plenty of power—than to seek the seemingly perfect winner that may cost you many more points than it will win.

Stefan Edberg

MYTH:	**Move forward on your serve.**
FACT:	**Top players hit up on the serve, then fall forward.**

Pushing forward with the body on the serve causes a tendency to hit down with the arm. Visually, it seems that you have to hit down to get speed on a serve. But the more you hit down the more you have to open the racket to get the ball over the net, and the ball gets backspin instead of topspin, losing its downward curve.

At the high speeds of professional tennis the ball has to have some topspin, even in the hardest serves, both for accuracy and consistency. To get that, the body needs to go up to help the arm to fully extend *past* the impact with the ball.

Most professionals hit upward on their serve, but sometimes it is not enough. I recall spending less than an hour with Robbie Seguso at the beginning of his professional career. I had him standing on the service line facing the back fence, serving a bucketful of balls on the condition that he hit them over the fence but with plenty of topspin.

In the beginning he hit several balls into the fence and he was slightly puzzled. He thought he was hitting up, but obviously it was not up enough.

He continued until he got every ball over the fence. We picked up the balls, then he served normally.

It took him a few minutes to adjust, but soon I saw a miracle. He had raised his serving to an incredible level of speed, depth, accuracy, and kick.

He had all the talent. Once he got the right concept and feel, he could do no wrong.

Partnered with Ken Flach, Seguso's serve, together with their other assets, got them to the position of #1 doubles team in the world.

This upward effort is even more pronounced on second serves. Hitting upward on the second serve instead of hitting forward helps to get the ball into the service court, with both speed and spin.

Rather than slowing down your swing, pull it upward even faster than your first serve, like Boris Becker and Stefan Edberg, brushing up on the ball. As a result, you'll get an "American Twist" serve, a pronounced topspin shot that will clear the net by a couple of feet or more and land prior to the service line. The ball may look slow at first, but it will kick fast and high.

Players who don't have this action either slow down their second serve or they risk a lot, while a good "American Twist" server doesn't slow down the motion at all and feels plenty of power and confidence on the second serve.

Jim Courier

> *MYTH:* **Put your left foot across to hit your forehand.**
>
> *FACT:* **Open stance forehands are more powerful and natural.**

The greatest forehands of modern time—Manuel Santana's, Borg's, Lendl's, Graf's, Agassi's, and Courier's—are definitely open stance.

Those professionals don't care which foot they land on, but most often hit their forehand with their feet facing the net. Not only does this help them stroke, but it also allows them to come back quicker to the middle to cover the court. While it is almost impossible to hit a good topspin forehand from a very closed stance, the opposite is true with a very open stance.

You may turn your shoulders if you feel more comfortable or more power this way, but that is as far as you need to go.

That is why at the start of your forehand lessons in this book you are facing the net, oblivious to the position of your feet, while in most formal lessons the student is put sideways to the net and made to step forward with the left foot.

Sports science could well look into the fact that hand-eye coordination is totally dependent on the athlete's attention on coordinating the hand with his visual perception of the motion of the ball. The rest of the body gets coordinated to the movement of the hand in a natural, instinctive way, without the athlete's mental effort.

As a very simple analogy, visualize yourself shaking hands with a very attractive Hollywood movie star and paying attention to the position of your feet, whether your weight is on the front foot or the back one, and several other details. I wonder whether you would even find his or her hand.

Hand-eye coordination means, by definition, precisely that, HAND-EYE, not hand-eye-foot-weight coordination. The methods in this book are based on the simple discovery that to improve your hand-eye coordination, whether you are a beginner, an advanced player, or a pro, you have to focus entirely on the contact between racket and ball.

This does not mean that a player does not have a favorite position in which he feels most comfortable, or balanced, or powerful. But he has worked it out through feel, in an instinctive way, not through words or mental commands.

While you are playing it is a good idea to keep your feet moving, shuffling, or skipping, to keep your legs alert and ready to start. But don't disturb your focus by thinking about your feet. Keep your attention on the ball, on finding it, on the contact and then on the finish of the stroke.

Boris Becker

> *MYTH:* **Keep your distance from the ball—usually ''an arm's length.''**
>
> *FACT:* **Closer distances are better for power and for control.**

How did you catch something thrown to you when you were a kid? Did you run to get as close to it as possible and then extend your arm to catch it, or did you try to keep your distance? You got as close as possible. Most conventional tennis techniques make you keep your distance while running. But very advanced tournament players or pros try to get their head or eyes close to the line of flight of the ball when they run. Then they slow down and hit the ball at their side.

Michael Chang

> *MYTH:* **Keep your arm straight on your forehand.**
>
> *FACT:* **Bending the arm on the forehand is much more natural.**

On the forehand swing, it is easier to adjust your distance to the ball by bending the arm, just like when you shake hands. It also gives you more power, since you are using the biceps muscle, one of the strongest in the body.

For hard topspin shots, the racket face needs to come over the ball, preventing it from sailing out. This is more easily done by bending the arm at the elbow, rather than keeping it straight.

Stefan Edberg

> *MYTH:* **Step forward into the ball.**
>
> *FACT:* **Top pros emphasize lifting, not stepping forward.**

Tennis is basically a vertical game. You need to get the ball to clear the net, then drop into the court.

In your topspin strokes you want much more of a lift than forward power, both to clear the net and to get the ball to rotate.

In the topspin forehand, there is a natural tendency to go forward with the right side of the body while pulling up. In the two-handed backhand, likewise, the left side tends to go forward. Those are forceful upper body turns and lifting that get power into the shot.

Stepping forward or backward is a function of your adjustment to the ball. If the ball is short, you move in. If the ball is deep, you may move back.

Steffi Graf

MYTH: **Stay down through the stroke.**

FACT: **It is more natural to pull up.**

Under normal circumstances, staying down may trap your swing rather than facilitate it.

If the ball is short, low, or you are meeting it far in front, you may need to stay down to reach it.

Making a player stay down for every shot is a major block to his or her improvement. Top players develop a "feel" for the optimum move in a particular situation, staying down for some shots, coming up for others.

This is true even for the backhand slice, where lifting the shoulder by lifting up the trunk helps extend the arm for the follow-through.

Gabriela Sabatini

> *MYTH:*   **Don't let your body go back.**
>
> *FACT:*   **The body does whatever is needed to make the shot.**

Many good players and professionals purposefully pull back in order to get more topspin. It adds to the safety factor of the shot, pulling the ball over the net and making it go down sooner on the other side.

In some shots, if you feel too close, pull back when you hit. This will give you comfortable distance from the ball, good control, and added topspin rotation.

The arm feels lighter and more powerful pulling up. You also feel that you have plenty of time during and after the stroke, and your

John McEnroe

racket stays up at the end a fraction longer. Look at Gabriela Sabatini's topspin backhand. What a beautiful thing!

> *MYTH:* **On your forehand, keep your racket head above your wrist all the time.**
>
> *FACT:* **Any top pro drops the racket head below the ball and below the hand at some point in their swing.**

This is true especially on balls hit below waist level.

Even on high topspin shots the racket head sometimes gets below the hand.

From Laver to Borg, to McEnroe, to Lendl, the exceptions are very few. To hit from low to high you obviously have to be below the ball at some time, and the most comfortable and most effective way of doing it is to drop the racket head somewhere before the hit.

The more you drop it, the more you can come up and the more topspin you will have. The same goes for the two-handed backhand topspin stroke.

It doesn't matter whether you loop your stroke or go straight down and up. Just get below the ball and pull it up.

The opposite is true for the backhand slice and for volleys. You want to keep the racket head up longer so that you can come from high to low firmly. If the ball drops very low, the best way to get power and ball speed on these shots is to drop the racket head, as it goes forward with an open face, right before impact.

MYTH: **You can hit the ball harder flat than with topspin.**

FACT: **You can hit the ball harder flat, but right out of the tennis court!**

A flat 100 mph shot hit from net level or below from anywhere inside your court has no chance of landing inside your opponent's baseline, no matter how close to the top of the net you hit—unless you hit the net, your opponent, or a bird.

With enough topspin, you can hit a 100 mph shot in the court, with the same downward curve as a flat 60 mph shot.

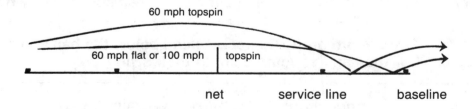

Topspin players like Borg, Lendl, Becker, and Agassi have hit forehands over 100 mph, *inside* their opponent's court, safely clearing the net.

Another consideration in hitting hard and flat is your chance of winning the point. At a high level of play, pros go for the percentage shots.

Let's say that you have a 50 percent chance if you are a pro (maybe 30 percent if you are an advanced club player) of hitting a flat 80 mph groundstroke to a corner. What if your opponent gets it back somehow? Would you take another chance like that?

Match results are determined more by unforced errors than by great shots. At a professional level, unless the court is slick and fast, the ball keeps coming back and coming back.

Those players are both forceful and safe.

There is a perception that the game has changed in the last few years, with top pros seeking to finish the point from the baseline in a very forceful way. This held true in earlier decades as well. Heavy topspin hitters like Borg and Lendl always relished finishing the point with a powerful shot, while still preserving their safety with the spin on the ball.

Today's powerful rackets have made the job easier. New equipment accounts for tremendous ball velocity, and topspin players can hit hard winners while still focusing on landing the ball safely in the court.

If you want to kill the ball with a groundstroke, blast it with topspin, looking like a tennis pro (or at least an approximation) rather than a baseball player.

MYTH: **Bend your knees only.**

FACT: **Top players bend whatever or wherever is natural.**

Combined with *stay down through the stroke,* only bending the knees makes players look like broken puppets. Bend naturally—waist, knees, arms—looking like an athlete, not like a stiff marionette.

Monica Seles

> *MYTH:*   **Move to the ball with sidesteps, then turn and hit.**
>
> *FACT:*   **Top pros pivot to run to the ball.**

Stepping sideways to run to the ball is the most ridiculous teaching method I ever saw. It makes players look like puppets. Players who were making good progress playing a natural way can have their coordination, timing, focus on finding the ball, and their feel destroyed by a teacher who gets them to move in that way.

Top players sometimes sidestep while they are waiting to see their opponent's next shot, or when the ball is right there and they want to keep their open stance. But to purposely sidestep to run to a distant ball is crazy.

There is nothing more natural, more graceful and more efficient than turning toward wherever you are going and taking a few steps, leaning in that direction, gently, nonchalantly.

One of the greatest pros who has ever played that way was Ilie Nastase. He looked the smoothest, he was called the fastest ever, but all he did was lean and turn perfectly in the direction he wanted to go. He seemed to have ages to get to the ball. He wasn't the quickest, he just had perfect moves.

MYTH: **¼-turn grip rotation between forehand and backhand.**

FACT: **No grip change is necessary for the two-handed backhand. For the one-handed backhand, pros bring the racket parallel to the body to change grip, rather than just rotating it.**

If you have a two-handed backhand you don't need to rotate the grip at all. The right hand can keep the forehand grip, while the left hand does most of the work throughout.

If your backhand is one-handed, the technique is different. You need to change your forehand grip to a backhand grip to get better racket support at impact time. The racket moves to a position parallel to the front of your body, together with your shoulder turn to the left, while your grip slides inside your right hand, changing position.

This change occurs primarily in the bottom portion of the hand, closest to the little finger, while the fingers go from a spread-out position on the forehand grip to a close together position for the flat backhand grip.

Not as much grip rotation occurs between your index finger and thumb. But the palm of the hand has come on top of the top portion of the racket grip to achieve a more perpendicular position of the arm to the racket. This gives you much better support while hitting topspin, too.

You can test this grip by pressing the racket flat against a wall or a tennis court fence, as if you were contacting the ball with your backhand. If your grip is okay, you'll feel plenty of support for your push.

For the one-handed backhand slice the grip change from forehand to backhand is much smaller, and the fingers stay spread apart. Here a ⅛-turn or grip rotation would be more accurate, but this change is always larger toward the little finger than toward the index finger.

(Feel your grip, rather than looking at it. Looking at your grip and constantly worrying over having the correct grip takes valuable attention away from finding the ball.)

(Shown facing the net →)

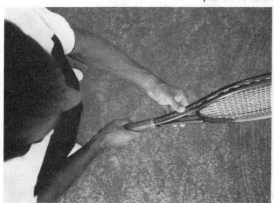

Forehand grip

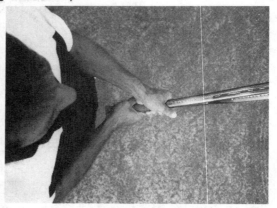

Two-handed backhand grip

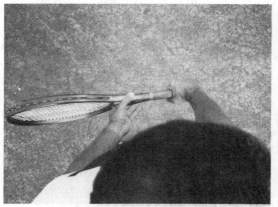

Topspin or flat backhand grip

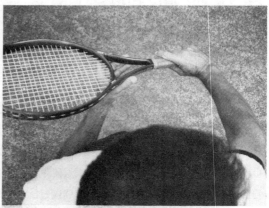

Slice backhand grip

Michael Chang

> ***MYTH:*** **Point your racket toward your aim at the end of the fore-hand stroke.**
>
> ***FACT:*** **The racket comes across the body.**

Pointing the racket toward the target makes for a straight arm forehand. The opposite—bending the arm—will give you more power, control, and topspin, and you'll be able to better close the racket face angle.

You'll also prevent undue stress on your arm, and you'll have better balance and momentum to turn back toward the center of the court after your shot.

The same is true for the two-handed backhand. Bend both arms toward your right shoulder to achieve a full topspin swing.

As for the sliced two-handed backhand or a chip, your right arm may be more dominant and straighten itself.

In the one-handed backhand it is true that the right arm will finish pointing approximately to the target, whether it is a topspin shot, where the arm will finish high, or a slice, where the arm will finish low. But the wrist will never "break" to have the racket point in that direction, too. The racket will end up in an angle approximately perpendicular to the arm, whether it goes over (topspin), or under the ball (slice).

MYTH: **Topspin is more stressful for your arm.**

FACT: **Flat shots impact the arm harder.**

Although topspin requires more physical effort overall than conventional tennis, it distributes the stress impact over a wider area.

A ball coming at you and met squarely ("flat" in tennis jargon), puts the stress on your arm and tends to turn your body. You need to tighten your grip substantially, as well as your arm and shoulder, to put force into your swing.

Because of gravity, which affects your body as well as the ball, some of the impact force gets dissipated through your body and pushes you toward the ground. On flat shots, this gives the feeling that your feet are firmly planted on the ground.

The topspin shot, on the other hand, is an upward movement. Your force is actually counteracting gravity. You feel light on your feet, sometimes coming off the ground. The force of the incoming ball gets dissipated or canceled by your upward force. It may tend to ground you, but since you are pulling up anyway, you don't feel it as much as in the flat strokes.

Not twisting with your feet grounded saves your lower back from much torsion stress. Of course you have to bend down, then pull up in your topspin shots. Sometimes you jump, even while on the run. But these movements are truly natural, nothing that humans haven't done for millions of years.

Andre Agassi

With topspin, the stress on the arm is diminished by the fact that the impact is also dissipated into spin. The incoming ball travels downward on your racket strings, while you are pulling up.

You can hit a hard topspin shot without having to lock up on the racket with your hand. The racket path or angle doesn't get disturbed much even if your grip is quite loose, which shows the efficiency of the technique.

On the contrary, with a flat shot you need to tighten your grip or your racket may fly in some other direction than your shot. Those are the forces that you counter by tightening up your hand, your arm, and by planting your feet firmly on the ground.

In a very graphic way, hitting hard topspin shots feels like taking off in an airplane. By comparison, hitting forceful flat shots feels like crashing to the ground.

> *MYTH:* **You have to hit deep.**
>
> *FACT:* **The deeper you try to drive the ball during rallies, the more mistakes you'll make.**

Ivan Lendl

Unless you are hitting an approach shot, where depth may be critical, you have to hit the ball in the court consistently.

The deeper you try to drive the ball during rallies, the more mistakes you'll make. The ball may go much deeper than intended, overshooting your opponent's baseline.

Over 80 percent of the groundstrokes at the top professional level bounce closer to the service line than the baseline.

Just clearing the service line is enough *intended* depth. If the ball goes deeper, it will still land in the court.

I have seen a great champion of our time, Ivan Lendl, start a match without much confidence, and coolly and safely keep the ball in play with plenty of topspin. He would hit high-looping strokes, mixed with a few sliced backhands, nothing too close to the lines.

He'd work himself into the match, grinding his way into his opponent's resistance. Then, as the match progressed, perhaps with a set under his belt, he would steamroll his opponent, hitting powerfully all over the court. Wonderful, wonderful topspin, so powerful yet so safe!

Bjorn Borg has won innumerable matches and championships doing just that on his groundstrokes, hitting the ball harder than anyone of his time. Only Jimmy Connors had comparable ball speed due to his special rackets and taking the ball on the rise.

Boris Becker is another of the great topspin players of all time. Depth is not critical for him, but his power drives a high percentage of his shots deep.

He had tremendous topspin on both sides at a young age. He is not totally a percentage player now, since he loves the power that can pull him out of difficulty—or get him into it—at any time.

Becker is the most complete player of the current generation, and perhaps the most exciting to watch. He can switch from safety to power, then to touch shots, in the blink of an eye. Sometimes he elects to tough it out from the baseline. Other times he storms the net right from the start of the point.

He is undoubtedly a perfect example of the modern game: tremendous power tamed with topspin.

These great players' success obviously depends on the mixture of power and control. At high speeds, and with the newly developed wide body rackets, to hit the ball flat makes for more errors. That is true even at the net, as shown by Becker's problems with his forehand volley, perhaps his least efficient stroke.

A backspin on your volleys, even if minimal, will add to your control, to your "feel" of the ball.

Stefan Edberg

From the backcourt it is the same story, rolling the ball the other way. The more topspin, no matter how hard you hit, the sooner the ball will drop.

If you want to hit the ball deeper in a rally, hit it harder, or higher. Keep hitting with enough topspin and it will land in front of your opponent's baseline and jump. You'll be risking less than if you flatten out your shots to get more depth, and your shots will be harder for your opponent to return.

Conclusion

Take a new, fresh look at the pros. Instead of watching the ball going back and forth, fix your eyes on the player of your choice. Watch his moves—how he prepares, when he starts to stroke, how he hits the ball, his follow-through, the finish, how he goes back to the middle, everything he does, and most importantly, how he finds the ball.

Not every pro plays topspin, and very few do it every single shot. Jimmy Connors, for example, has some different strokes.

Connors twists his serve with plenty of overspin (American Twist), but he hits the groundstrokes rather flat. He has perhaps the best return of serve ever, and he excels at hitting on the rise.

He is also superb at finding the ball. Here is the example of a great player *pushing* his groundstrokes with ball speeds sometimes exceeding 100 mph. Aided formerly by a steel racket with a wire suspension system for the strings, he was able to almost touch the ball with the racket, then he would accelerate with the ball in his strings. The racket had a trampoline effect that gave him at least 20 percent more ball speed than the best rackets of that time.

He was the only pro who could master that racket. He played with it for many years after it became obsolete, collecting used rackets from friends and fans to stock up his supply.

Finally he switched to a modern racket frame, and although still a fabulous player, his strokes lost some of their incredible former sting.

Keep your eyes fixed on Connors while he plays and you'll see why he is so good. Observe how slowly his racket approaches the ball before going "boom." The chances of him mis-hitting the ball are almost nil, and his placements depend only on the racket angle at impact time.

Jimmy Connors

You'll see him accelerating from the ball forward and finishing high. It is the natural path of his arms. His racket covers the ball to some extent, preventing it from shooting up. He may get the ball to rotate forward, but it is only a slight roll. He also gets some sideways rotation on the ball.

John McEnroe and Martina Navratilova are also masters at finding the ball, whether on their forehand, backhand, half volley, volleys or smash. Even on their serve, not only do they have power, but also wonderful control.

Their body movements help them find the ball particularly well. You see them pulling up, sometimes jumping up, on their volleys, on their groundstrokes, on their serve.

Very seldom will you see their body getting in the way. They are helping their playing hand to execute any shot they want.

Martina Navratilova

John McEnroe

These top players are all great athletes, but not superhuman. Their technique is obviously the most important factor contributing to their success.

There is no reason to teach a beginner or an advanced player in opposition to how the top pros play and claim that it is the right way to learn the game. On the contrary, using the same basic principles as the best players speeds up the learning process, it's more relaxing, and helps to make the game more enjoyable.

3

How to Correct Faulty Strokes

Do you have trouble with some aspects of your game? Do you want to correct or change some of your strokes? Then limit your correction to one stroke at a time, perhaps the one that you mis-hit the most or make more errors with.

Work on that one until it feels much better before you start on anything else.

If you work on several strokes at the same time, it may disrupt your game and make you feel like you are going in several directions at the same time.

What is preferable is the feel of the improvement on a particular area, the desired change that boosts your confidence. Stated clearly, it is best to narrow down the area in which you are working. Then, when that stroke becomes grooved-in and steady, you can tackle another one, and so on.

There are two major ways of correcting a stroke:

1) Find out which basic thing you are doing wrong and work on that, getting the missing pieces in one by one.

For example, let's say that in reading this book you realize that you prepare too soon on your forehand, taking your racket back too early.

To correct that, get a friend to hit only slow, high-looping balls to your forehand. Wait longer and longer than usual before taking your racket back.

The ball will bounce, getting close to you. Perhaps you have already turned your shoulders, but keep both hands on the racket to prevent it from going back too early. Then swing, accelerating from the contact point on and emphasizing the end of the stroke over your left shoulder.

Do this until you lose your panic over stroking too late.

Of course, you may have hit several balls too late, but you also find out how long you can wait. Adjust accordingly, always waiting and stressing the finish of the stroke. By now, it should be a different feel altogether.

Next, work on relating the end of the swing to your placement, as described in Chapter Seven on forehand, perhaps doing the drills around the can.

Repeat these drills until you are sure of this new feel, until you are used to it, until you like it, until you are confident about it. By now the ball should be going exactly where you want.

The same procedure would work, for example, if you feel you need more topspin. Drop the racket head below the ball, then come up over your left shoulder, brushing up on the ball instead of hitting the ball squarely.

Again, exaggerate the topspin in the beginning to get a better idea of what it feels like. Here the string above the net described in Chapter Seven would be a good aid. It will make you pull up farther on your stroke and give you the idea that if you don't get enough roll on the ball it will go out long.

Now you could pick up some other drills from Chapter Seven, or from "Drills for Development," Chapter Sixteen, and practice those until you feel comfortable and confident with your topspin stroke.

Pick up bits and pieces of information in this book. Write them down.

Work on one thing at a time. If you keep it simple and objective, you will come out at the other end with flying colors.

2) The other way to correct a stroke is to start from scratch. Turn to the chapter on the one-handed backhand (Chapter Nine), for example, and go through the whole learning process and each drill, for as long as is needed.

It is very important to start at very low ball speeds, both for the "feed" from your friend or teacher, and for your hit.

At these low speeds you'll be more aware of the movement and how your force gets transferred into ball speed. At high speeds this difference won't be as noticeable as at lower speeds.

There is definitely a different feel between accelerating from the ball forward (push), and accelerating prior to the impact (hit).

On groundstrokes, it should feel like slow motion prior to contact with the ball. Then you accelerate.

The same technique should be applied for your harder hits. Your racket should approach the ball slowly, then you explode from the impact on.

By practicing this way you may be sacrificing some ball speed at first, but you'll be gaining lots of control and understanding.

It will be easier to see why the ball goes in one direction or another, higher or lower, faster or slower, rotating or not.

You are also developing racket sensitivity, awareness of what you are causing and why.

You can choose either method of correction, depending on your advancement and your idea of what you want to accomplish.

Which Basics Are Wrong?

You can find out which basics are wrong by comparison.

You probably have an ideal stroke in mind, perhaps a stroke from some great player. Compare that to your stroke.

First look for differences in timing. When does he start his swing? How long does he wait? How close is the ball when he commits his swing?

Many times the path of the racket is dictated by the way you find the ball. The time you start your swing definitely influences the way you find it.

The most disruptive thing of all is to start your stroke too soon. The racket will start on a swing pattern, then, when you are already stroking, you see how the ball has bounced as it comes toward you.

Now you need to make corrections midway through your swing. This can severely disrupt your stroke pattern. Subsequent corrections to your swing won't straighten out the real problem because it doesn't lie there, but in your timing.

It is far better to wait until after the bounce of the ball to start your swing because then you know where the ball is really going. You'll also get to know the "too late" boundary, something that you may have been totally unaware of.

People that are constantly afraid of "being late" may be consistently early. In tennis, this results in inconsistency.

This difference in timing may be very small, especially at high ball speeds, but it definitely changes your approach to the ball.

The key is to "feel" that you are waiting, instead of trying to get ready as soon as you see the ball coming your way.

Slowly you'll become aware that you can time your groundstroke to the bounce of the ball, not to your opponent's hit.

Once this is corrected the stroke usually becomes easier, more natural, more effective, and you get more feel.

It doesn't mean that you'll need less force, because pushing can be a greater effort than hitting. You are accelerating the racket with the ball already there, while in a hit you may actually be throwing the racket at the ball. But with correct timing and technique the stroke will feel smooth.

Your efficiency and accuracy are in direct ratio to correct timing and technique. Therefore, the timing is the first important detail you should focus on.

Here is a list of some of the things you can check out when you have problems with a particular stroke:

1) Check your grip by pressing your racket flat against a vertical surface, like a fence or a wall, to see if you have good support of the racket.

Although many topspin shots are hit leading the shot with the racket's upper edge, some kind of support for the impact on the strings is necessary for the shot to be truly effective.

To test the grip for your backhand slice and your volleys, push with the bottom edge of the racket, angled at 45 degrees to the wall.

2) Do you start your swing too early?

On groundstrokes, do you wait for the bounce of the ball?

3) Do you focus on finding the ball, or are you focusing on something else?

4) Does it feel like you hit behind the ball, or that you hit from the ball forward?

5) Do you follow through just by the momentum of the early part of your stroke, or do you deliberately accelerate toward the end of your swing?

6) Does it feel like you finish the stroke in the same place all the time, independent of where you hit the ball, or does your finish vary?

7) Do you concentrate on finding the ball and then the "finish" of your stroke, or are you thinking of your footwork or something else?

8) On your groundstrokes, do you sweep your hand smoothly through the stroke, or do you make sudden changes in racket angle, disturbing its path?

Usually more than one of these problems shows up, as one thing done poorly induces problems in several other areas.

Basic errors are compounded with compensations dreamed up to somehow get the ball into the court.

For example:

1) An incorrect grip makes a stroke awkward.

2) A too-early preparation usually causes tightness and stiffness during the stroke.

3) Not focusing on finding the ball causes lots of mis-hits.

4) Hitting behind the ball rather than from the ball forward causes loss of control. The result is a tentative followthrough.

5) Not finishing the same groundstroke in the same place will give you a different stroke for every occasion. You will then have to resort to adjusting the racket angle differently each time, plus make adjustments for ball speed, height, spin, etc. This actually makes for hesitations, especially under pressure.

Most of these examples are for groundstrokes.

The volley has a completely different feel. As your body goes for the ball, you wait till the ball is near to discharge your shot, stopping your hand at contact with the ball.

By correcting one or two things that are basic, everything else should fall into place.

I can only generalize in this chapter, because there are many ways of swinging, and few ways of hitting the ball really effectively.

Overall, the most important thing is to get the ball in the court.

You may think you have beautiful strokes, but if the balls don't land consistently inside the court, nobody will get to admire your game at Wimbledon or on TV—or in the finals of your club tournament.

In other words, *consistency* is the name of this game.

Mats Wilander has been a prime example of consistency. Midway through the 1980s he was probably the player who made the least errors in a match.

He could go for several games without an unforced error. He hit his first serve with spin, not with overwhelming power, but consistently in.

By 1988 he had developed an excellent backhand slice and some good volleying to add to his flawless topspin strokes. Now he coupled his groundstroke steadiness with good excursions to the net on important points. He waited for the shorter ball to attack and he didn't miss approach shots either.

All these assets, plus his superb conditioning and speed, got him three Grand Slam* tournament titles that year and he shot to #1 in the world.

Borg, Lendl, Wilander, Becker, Agassi, Courier, and Michael Chang are all classic examples of the modern topspin game.

So is McEnroe, who as a youngster was a strong topspin player, and also great on slow clay courts. He later adjusted his game and his grip to the faster surfaces and became mostly a serve-and-volley player, but retained his great touch and control on his groundstrokes.

Few players have combined great groundstrokes with tremendous prowess at the net. In that sense, McEnroe and Laver are the most complete players of the modern era, and Becker is quickly approaching that stage. Becker's only trouble spot is his low forehand volley, which he hits too flat.

If you want a powerful and efficient game, these are some of the players who could stand as an example for you. I would not hesitate to include Graf's forehand, Evert's two-handed backhand, Navrati-

*Grand Slam: Wimbledon, The U.S., French, and Australian Opens.

lova's serve and volleys, Sabatini's topspin backhand, and Seles's groundstrokes, in the greatest strokes in the game, male or female.

We always have a favorite. Sometimes we admire a stroke from one player, another stroke from someone else. A careful analysis can find the differences between your stroke and the ones you think are the best.

Working out which are the most important details to focus on may take some trial and error on the practice court.

If you are an advanced player, you may have a lot of data already. You get all this new data and sometimes it seems hard to put it all together. The best way to make an important correction is to focus entirely on the new data for a while, and practice that particular shot.

After you adapt to the new feel and see the results regarding control and placement, go back to a very concerted effort on getting the ball in the court, thinking of nothing else.

The new data, if it is true and beneficial, should align itself with your past experience, provided you threw the misconceptions overboard.

If something goes wrong after some practice, focus on the new data again and work on it a while longer. The errors should diminish with more practice time.

It is very hard to push erroneous data on a very good player. He would be very unhappy after a few tries. Again, the truth is simple. Things either work or they don't. Your accuracy and consistency will either improve or it will not.

You may test something new for a while, but if it doesn't give you more feel and control, drop it by the wayside.

To improve the feel of your stroke and also as a warm-up exercise you can attach a weight to your racket (see pictures on next page). Use this weight to mimic your strokes, without hitting the ball.

The "Swing Master™"

By swinging with this weight attached to your racket, all the way through to the end of your stroke, you'll become aware of your natural stroke path, the one that doesn't require unusual forces that disturb the racket angle and therefore your control.

At some point close your eyes and swing slowly at first, then accelerate from the imagined impact point to the end of the stroke, feeling your arm all the way. Keep repeating it until you get used to that feeling of power from the imaginary point of contact to the end of the stroke.

On the topspin forehand stroke, for example, the increased weight of the racket will make you feel the work of your biceps muscle as it pulls the racket over your left shoulder. You'll learn to use the forces of nature to your advantage, rather than fight them with an unnatural or mechanical swing.

You may also notice that lifting your body helps you accelerate the racket on its way up. Learn not to resort to sudden turns or jerking motions, but to a strong lift.

On other shots some different data will turn up. You'll get a "feeling" for which is the best way to stroke.

The end result of this type of practice is increased feeling. When you take the weight off and start stroking the ball, your racket will feel light. If you have practiced properly, accelerating your groundstrokes from impact on, your timing will not be affected. On the contrary, it will reinforce the feel of finding the ball first, then hitting from the ball on.

On volleys, the increased weight can be used to reinforce the stopping action. Much power and control is gained after you take the weight off, but only if you time volleys properly and stop at contact with the ball.

Another good exercise is to practice your strokes in front of a big mirror. Look at the mirror, not at your hand. Imagine finding the ball first, touching it, and then watch yourself accelerate to the end of the stroke.

When you get back to the court try to slow things down, at least in your mind. Your eyes are focused on the ball, your other senses are focused on "feeling" it.

The mechanics may be important, but what will help you remember and repeat a stroke is what it feels like.

Repeating a stroke slowly and deliberately, all the way to the end, will register it both at your conscious and your instinct level, allowing you to call on the information at any time.

After a while you'll hit the ball instinctively the same way whether the ball is fast or slow. As long as you don't panic and rush your shot, the same feel will take over.

You may not have time to figure it all out consciously, but the "feel" will be the same.

Then, when somebody asks you about your groundstrokes, somehow show this "feel." With your hand or your racket show how you carry, how you push the ball.

On volleys, show how you stop your hand and direct the ball.

Rather than going for lengthy explanations about the mechanics of your stroke, talk about the "good stuff," which is nothing more than that tennis is a game of "feel," not of complicated thought.

4

Basics and Definitions

The Racket

The development of the large tennis racket has made tennis much easier to learn and to play. Many top professionals use oversized rackets, with head sizes of up to 110 square inches. In these rackets the string area of lively response, called the "sweet spot," is several times larger than in the old racket types.

Read Chapter Eighteen, "Rackets and Balls," if you need help choosing a racket.

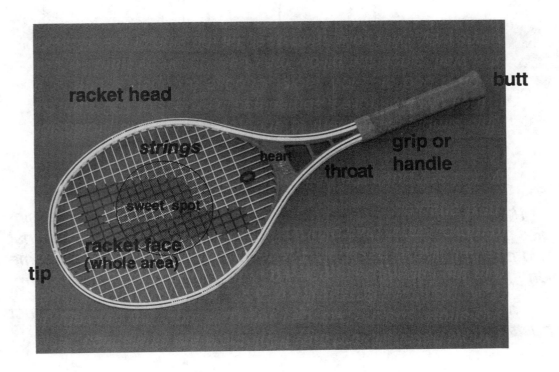

The Court

The tennis court is 27 feet wide by 78 feet long (both sides in-cluded), for singles play, that is, one player playing against one other player.

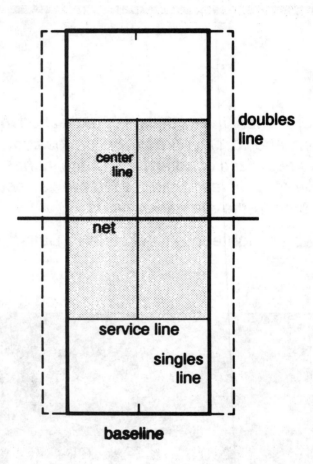

The heavy lines in the diagram show the boundaries of the sin-gles court. The doubles court is used when two players play against two other players. It includes the singles court and it is the same length but 4½ feet wider on each side (dotted lines in the diagram).

The net is 3 feet high in the center and 3½ feet high at the net posts.

The main purpose of the game is to get the ball over the net and into your opponent's court.

The Groundstrokes: Forehand and Backhand

Only one bounce of the ball is allowed in your court before you return it over the net. Those strokes hit after the bounce of the ball are called the "groundstrokes."

> **NOTE:** THE TECHNIQUES IN THIS BOOK ARE EXPLAINED FOR A PERSON WHO IS RIGHT-HANDED.
>
> IF YOU ARE LEFT-HANDED, THE TECHNIQUES ARE JUST THE OPPOSITE, LIKE A MIRROR IMAGE.

When the ball comes to your right side and you stroke it, this is called a "forehand" shot because your stroke is led by the fore, or *front part of your right hand. When the ball comes to your left side and you stroke it, that is called a "backhand" shot (whether you do it with one or with both hands on your racket), because the stroke is led with the back side of your right hand.*

The Serve

The first hit in any point is called a "serve." The player having his turn at serving stands behind his baseline and has to hit the first ball, the serve, into the service court (shaded area in the next diagram).

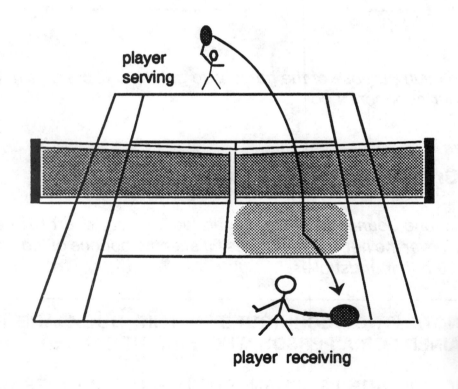

player serving

player receiving

The receiver may not return the serve before it bounces. There are four service courts, indicated in the first court diagram of this chapter by the thinner lines and shaded areas.

There is more information on the serve and the service sequence in Chapter Ten.

The Volleys and Smash

You may retrieve the ball before it bounces in your court, as long as it has cleared the net, except in the return of serve. When you hit the ball before it bounces your shot is called a "volley." If the ball comes to your right side it is a "forehand volley." If it comes to your left side, it is a "backhand volley."

If the ball is coming well above you and you strike it directly overhead, your shot is called an "overhead" or a "smash."

This game in the frontcourt is called "the net game," or "the volley game."

Basic Concepts

The net is the main barrier between you and your opponent's court. Since gravity pulls the ball down at all times, you need to lift the ball over the net most of the time, especially from the backcourt. That requires an upward pull as you stroke the ball, rather than just a forward motion.

You could achieve the same effect by opening the racket face, but the combination of an upward pull and an open racket face usually sends the ball flying off the court.

The Flight of the Ball

The tennis ball can fly from very low speeds up to approximately 150 mph in the hardest hits, but it usually travels around or under 50 mph in any rally.

Because of the size and the covering, the ball slows down considerably during flight. A player at one baseline hits a ball, for exam-

ple, at 60 mph. By the time it bounces and gets to the opponent's baseline, especially on slow courts, it may be going 25 mph or less.

A player, standing behind the baseline, sees his opponent hitting the ball from the backcourt. Let's say the ball went to a height of 9 feet while crossing the net. He sees the ball curve down and bounce in his court, then come up to about six feet and start dropping again. This second curve is much smaller than the first curve and considerably slower (see illustration).

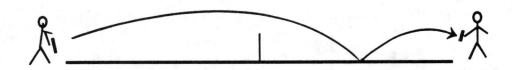

A slower ball coming from a shorter distance would look like this:

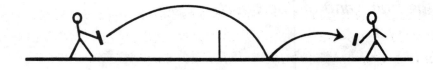

A tennis player needs to get used to these curves. In Chapter Five there are drills that develop familiarity with these curves, and the player's coordination and timing.

Racket Angle

The pros control the height of their shots with the racket angle. You can tilt the racket backwards, which we call "opening" the racket face, or you can tilt it forward, which we call "closing" the racket face.

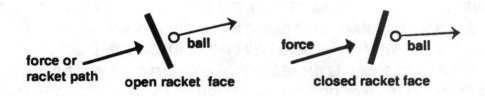

These changes in racket angle are all done without any changes in your grip of the racket. They are just different ways of angling the hand, as if you were, for example, turning the hand upward to catch something falling, or downward to catch something coming up.

An open racket face will send the ball much higher. A closed racket face will send the ball much lower. A small difference in the racket face angle can vary the height of your shot quite dramatically. This will become apparent during practice.

While you are a beginner and are playing the ball at slow speeds, your racket face should be slightly open. As you progress you'll need to close the racket face quite a bit. After some experience you'll learn to work this angle automatically, according to the height you want on each shot.

The racket angle determines also the direction of your shot. This is explained further in Chapter Seven, "The Forehand."

Very simply, the racket angle is the main factor in determining where the ball goes, rather than the swing.

The Push

The racket is about six times heavier than the ball, and sometimes hits the ball too fast and without control. That is why tennis professionals develop a very strong push on their groundstrokes, rather than a strong hit like in baseball. In this push the pros almost touch the ball with their racket before they start exerting force, so they have maximum control while still generating plenty of shot speed.

One of the drawbacks to learning tennis in the U.S. is that most people know baseball, and they think there are similarities between the tennis stroke and the baseball swing. In fact, they are very different. The tennis stroke is more like a push, with the force being generated from the impact point onward, rather than prior to the contact with the ball, like in baseball. The tennis groundstrokes are also an upward move, rather than a forward swing. This will become clearer in the next chapter.

Why do I say push the ball rather than hit it? Wouldn't you lose power?

Do this simple experiment to understand how the professionals "push" their groundstrokes, sometimes in excess of 100 mph. Stand a pillow on a bed or a low table. Choose an open space or do it against a wall, since the pillow may take off pretty hard and break things in its way. With your hand open hit the side of the pillow hard. Observe how far it moves. Stand the pillow up again. Now put your hand on the side of the pillow, barely touching it, then push it with forward and upward force.

Observe how far it moves. If you put any force to it, you can send the pillow half way across the room with the push, considerably more than the movement you got with your hit.

There will be more definitions and concepts as this book advances. So as not to bog down the beginner with a myriad of terms and ideas, I will leave them for the time they are needed.

Each chapter also has sections that amplify and explain the techniques for the more experienced player.

For tennis teachers and advanced players reading this book, Chapter Two on "Misconceptions" explains controversial ideas in more detail.

5

Checking and Developing Your Coordination

Coordination in tennis is basically getting to the ball as easily as possible and stroking it comfortably. Ideally you would get to the ball with a minimum of effort and you would exert yourself while stroking only as much as needed to make your shot safe and effective. In other words, no wasted effort.

Since you learned your basic moves at a very early stage in your life, there is no need to relearn them. On the contrary, doing things as naturally as you can will accelerate your learning process, making it easier.

The forehand stroke in tennis is quite similar to catching the ball underhand and then releasing it with an underhand throw over the net and into your opponent's court. To coordinate your catch with the flight of the ball, you need to get your hand near the ball and wait until it gets to your fingers to grab it. If you rush, closing your fingers before the ball gets there, you'll miss the catch. If you don't find the ball well, you'll also miss the catch.

The same goes for your strokes in tennis. If you want good control of your shots, you need to get your racket very close to the ball before releasing your power.

This is the most important fact for you to learn.

Regardless of the many details involved, when you catch a ball you don't think about your steps or other body movements. You just run and worry about catching it. To hit your strokes in tennis you approach the ball the same way, as if you were going to catch it.

We will refer to the above as **finding the ball.** This is the most important and most underrated factor in tennis. Without it, nobody plays well.

To develop this and your coordination I have a few drills that you can do bare-handed, by yourself or with someone else, at home, on the court, or anywhere. Even if you are good at it, do each drill a few times to become trained to the bounce and changing speeds of the ball.

If you have some difficulty, it is better to work on your coordination right here, in the beginning. Do not start learning to play until you feel a comfortable control of what you are doing with your hands and with the ball.

You may have to do some gentle running while doing these drills. Do things as slowly and as efficiently as you can, keeping your eyes and your attention focused on the ball in flight. If some balls are uncomfortably far for your reach, just let them go and pick them up later. The emphasis is on control and coordination, rather than speed.

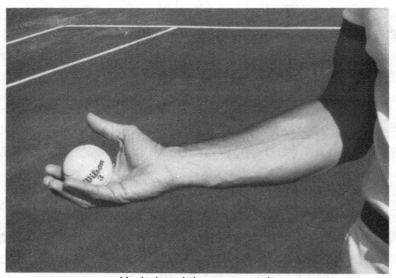

Underhand throw or catch

DRILL #1: *Toss the ball underhand higher than your head and catch it underhand on its way down. Repeat until you can catch the ball comfortably every time.*

DRILL #2: *Toss the ball underhand higher than your head. Let it bounce up, then, on its way down, catch it underhand. Repeat, tossing the ball to different heights, until you get a smooth catch each time.*

DRILL #3: *Toss the ball underhand against a wall. Let it come back, bounce up, and start to go down again. When it comes down to a comfortable height, perhaps a bit below waist level, catch it underhand. Do this at varying distances from the wall, ten feet away, twelve feet, and fifteen feet away. Also vary the height you hit on the wall.*

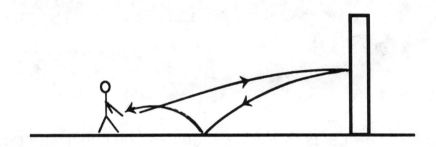

ALTERNATE DRILL #3: *If you are on the court or in an open space with another person have him or her toss the ball to you, at a distance of about 15 feet from each other.*

The ball should bounce well in front of you so that it starts to curve down, as shown in the illustration below. Catch it underhand, then throw it back underhand to the other person.

DRILL #4: *Same as Drill #3 or alternate Drill #3, except that instead of catching the ball you push it up with the palm of your hand (as shown on the next page) toward the other person, who catches*

it. If you are doing it against the wall, hit the ball once and catch it the next time. Repeat until you are accurate, both at finding the ball and sending it over the net.

Caution: For you beautiful ladies, this drill can break long fingernails if you miss the ball slightly.

DRILL #5: *Same as Drill #4, except that you finish your push over your left shoulder, touching it with your right index finger, as shown in the picture below.*

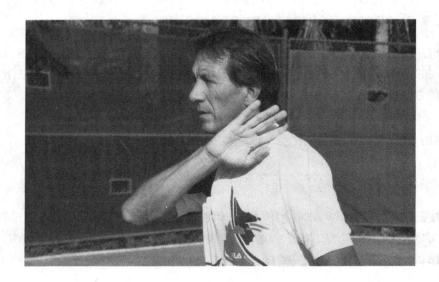

Your push should lift the ball to a height a little above your head, in the direction of the other person or the wall.

DRILL #6: *Play the ball back and forth with another person, both with the palm of your hands. Do it over something high, like a chair, or a few feet over the net if you are on a tennis court. Use the "over the shoulder" finish.*

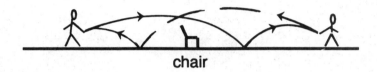

chair

If you are doing these drills against a wall by yourself, play it back and forth gently and pretty high, allowing yourself plenty of time between shots.

Repeat this last drill until you develop a rally (several hits back and forth). The emphasis should be on finding the ball all the time and having a controlled upward hit (or push) in the other's person direction.

By now, rather than rushing, you need to get your hand near the ball, a little below it, and to accelerate it from the contact point on upward. Even if your feet are rushing to get to the ball, your arm and hand need to move smoothly to find the ball, with all the effort applied from the contact point on.

The ball should reach an approximate height of six to eight feet in this drill, and should get to the other person comfortably after one bounce.

Again, if you don't have a partner, do these drills against a wall, keeping a comfortable distance to it, depending on the drill, and hit high enough to give yourself plenty of time between hits.

I have done these drills with many of my students. As a very interesting observation, I have found that those who had learned tennis the classic way, with body positioning and the like, have much more difficulty doing Drill #4 and the subsequent drills than a beginner unfamiliar with tennis instruction. The beginner would stroke the ball comfortably with the hand, while many accomplished players would miss the ball entirely. They would have an astonished look on their face, especially if they had seen the beginner doing it with ease. Those accomplished players had their attention drawn to how they were stroking the ball, rather than finding it. That apparently small diversion of their attention made them miss the ball.

6

Grip and Racket Position

The way you hold your racket in your hand for a particular shot is called your "grip."

Players usually have a "forehand grip," a "backhand grip," and some slight variations for serve and volleys.

Through the methods in this book grip changes become automatic, as part of the feel of each particular stroke.

To learn your basic grip and racket position put the racket on the ground at your right side, with the head of the racket pointing forward, as shown in this picture.

Grab the racket by the handle with your right hand and center the racket butt by your bellybutton, as shown below.

Look ahead—not at your racket. "Feel" the grip. Your fingers should be comfortable, slightly spread apart. The position of your hands can vary, according to your liking, and they might adjust themselves as you learn. The racket is pointing forward, level or slightly downward, and the racket face is fairly perpendicular to the ground.

The left hand is basically helping you rest your racket in both hands while are you not hitting the ball. This is formally called "the waiting position."

On a ball coming to your right side, the left hand will release the racket at some point after the bounce of the ball to let you swing at it. After the finish of the swing the racket will come back onto your left hand, again resting centered near your bellybutton.

On this basic grip and racket position, make sure the racket feels comfortable in your hands. I have purposely not shown the position of my right hand in the last picture because this varies from individual to individual. It is the player who chooses the exact grip, rather than the instructor doing it for the student. Choose what is most comfortable to you, not the teacher's idea of what is best for you.

Somewhere in the learning process small grip changes occur. This is okay, since the person is adjusting to a more comfortable, or more efficient grip.

That is in essence your forehand grip. There is nothing complicated about it. You don't need to think about it, and you don't need to look at it. It just needs to feel comfortable and secure.

You don't need to grip your racket tightly. Just keep it firm throughout the hit. You can vary the finger pressure accordingly, usually tightening up your fingers at impact time.

DRILL #1: After you learn the above, walk around the court, or your house, with the racket in both hands as described, until you get used to this position of your arms while you move around.

Turn to your right, walk, turn to your left, walk, then get to the middle of the court and face the net. Repeat a few times.

In a short while you'll be ready to play tennis. You need to keep your racket near your body while you are waiting or running, so that you aren't tempted to start your swing well before its time.

DRILL #2: At some point close your eyes while standing. Release you right hand from the grip and move it to the right side of your body, while keeping the racket in position with your left hand.

After a few seconds bring your right hand back onto the grip getting the same feel as before. This way you'll learn to find your grip without looking at it.

DRILL #3: After you developed certainty in the last drill, with your eyes still closed, release your right hand from the grip and move the racket toward the left side of your body with your left hand.

After a few seconds bring the racket back to your bellybutton and grip it again with your right hand, always feeling the same grip.

After a few repetitions do it with your eyes open, but without looking at your grip.

Just a few minutes doing each of these drills will groove-in your grip for life.

Backhand Grip

This two-hand resting position is also the basis for the two-handed backhand grip. In that stroke the driving hand is the left one, with the right hand accompanying the process, fairly relaxed, still keeping the forehand grip. The hands are fairly close, or touching each other, as shown below.

The power will be generated mostly by your left side.

Should you choose a one-handed backhand, your grip will be different. This is explained in Chapter Nine, "The One-Handed Backhand."

7

The Forehand

Let's say you are on a tennis court for the first time in your life. You've already done the coordination drills, and you are satisfied with your control of the ball. You also went through the chapter on basic grip and racket position and you should feel comfortable about that.

You brought a friend with you who is good at tossing the ball and you also brought a bucket of balls. A minimum of fifteen new or used balls would be good.

How Long to Play

You are about to learn your first stroke, the "forehand," through the ten drills in this chapter.

With some well-coordinated teenagers and adults, I have gotten through these drills in as short a time as thirty minutes. For others, it took well over an hour. Sometimes I would fit these drills into several half-hour lessons, done on different days.

I adjusted the lessons to the students' stamina, their physical conditioning, and the weather conditions.

You also need to manage your time on the court. Overdoing your first lesson could turn you off to tennis.

My suggestion is to spend one hour on the court at most the first day. For some very young children and unprepared adults, twenty minutes to half an hour would be enough.

When you come back on the court the next time, you can check back on some of the drills you did. Then proceed with the next few drills and so on.

How Long Should Each Drill Be?

Each student has a different speed of learning. You just have to do a drill until you are getting all the balls where you want and you have gotten the feel of the swing. In other words, do each drill until you are sure that you can repeat the swing at will and get the same results.

Warning

This is the moment when you are building those habits that will last for life. This book will tell you which things you need to focus on. Do nothing else, no matter how good somebody else's suggestions may seem at the time.

Most people are very generous with their advice, but they are not really knowledgeable about how to teach someone, no matter how well they play themselves.

With these methods you can learn in hours what it usually takes months to learn. But if this learning process is tampered with by introducing additions, your focus may change, and it may eventually disrupt your feel for the ball.

An Easy Way to Start

There are two ways you can start. One is with the racket full length, with the hand in the normal grip position, as shown in the

previous chapter. The other option is shortening the racket by hold-
ing it from somewhere in the throat, as shown above.

This is also called "choking" up on the racket, and the position of
your hand may vary according to your liking, and would be dependent on your success in controlling the ball.

The shorter you hold the racket, the easier it is to control the ball
when you are totally new to this sport. There is less of a tendency
this way to "swat" the ball, but as soon as you are hitting okay from
one position you can slide your hand back, gradually getting to the
normal grip position you learned in the previous chapter.

On the other hand, good athletes and well-coordinated people
can start from the normal grip position, but swinging slowly, avoiding
wild hitting and slapping the wrist.

Children should start with light rackets, much shorter than those
of an adult. You can get further information on shorter rackets in
Chapter Eighteen.

The Drills

First, for the sake of knowing how the ball bounces on the type of surface you are on, toss the ball back and forth with your friend, letting it bounce once each time. Then play it bare-handed over the net a few times, just like in the coordination drills.

Now, having done all that, grab your racket, centering it at your bellybutton as described in the last chapter. For an easy start, slide your right hand up on the racket.

Get in the middle of the court, six to ten feet in front of the service line, facing the net. Have your friend stand in the opposite court, near the net and to your left side. He should leave the middle of the court open for you to hit balls toward.

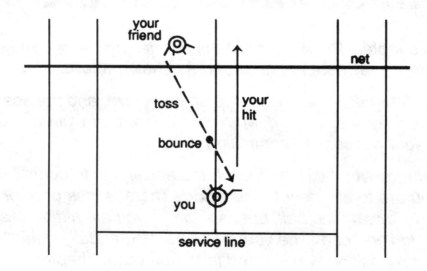

DRILL #1: Your friend feeds (tosses) a ball gently toward your right side. The ball should bounce well before it gets to you, allowing you plenty of time, just like in the hand drills. Wait for the ball to come near you, adjusting your body if necessary (Picture 1). Find the ball slowly and to your front with the center of your racket strings (Picture

2). Accelerate your right hand up and across your body until it touches the upper part of your left shoulder (Picture 3).

1   2   3

(Note: Start young children much closer to the net.)

Do this with a gentle upward pull as you touch the ball, creating the momentum of your arm from the ball forward, rather than prior to the contact with the ball. It should feel like you **pushed** the ball up and over the net.

First, find the ball well, as if you were going to grab it. As you touch the ball, accelerate your hand and racket mostly upward, bending your arm toward your left shoulder.

Your racket face is slightly open when you touch the ball, but you lead the swing with the upper edge of the racket, so that it goes up and over your left shoulder. This will propel the ball at about twenty mph, two to four feet over the net, in the direction of the open court. If the ball goes too high, close the racket face a bit for your next shot.

Do this drill fifty or sixty times starting from the racket in the belly-button position described earlier. After a while you'll start noticing *that the ball has a slight forward rolling action after leaving your racket. This is called topspin. The more you lift your arm, the more topspin you will get on the ball. Just two or three rolls of the ball until it bounces in the other court is enough topspin for you at this stage.*

Again, be gentle. Do not take a hard swing.

You can start to slide your hand toward a normal grip position, but keep the finish over the shoulder, whether you are "choking" up on the racket or not.

Note

How far to "choke" up on the racket depends on the person's strength and physical ability. Some people like to start with the hand closer to the throat of the racket, some others midway, and others would rather play with the hand on the racket's handle. It should be left to the student's discretion. A few tries, and you will know what feels best for you at the stage you are in.

Some people go through all the drills in this chapter gripping the racket short. This is perfectly all right. Confidence is built by success and the person knows instinctively what his "safety needs" are to get the ball on the racket and then into the other court.

Guidelines

Do not "break" your wrist. It can drastically affect the direction of your shot. The wrist is slightly laid back, with the racket's upper edge moving upward together with your arm.

Keep your focus on finding the ball and getting it over the net. Everything else will fall into place naturally as you do the drills in this chapter. You want to feel the ball on your strings as long as possible, and then to feel the finish of your stroke, as if these were the only important things to do.

Don't worry about the position of your body. Do whatever is comfortable for you. The less you do, the better. It's okay if your body faces the net, or if it's slightly turned. Just get those easy balls gently over the net, ending with your right hand over your left shoulder.

Many people make hitting the ball harder for themselves because they are also concentrating on the position of their feet, their balance, weight transfer, whether they are sideways to the net, their racket preparation, etc.

***Your focus** needs to stay on **finding** the ball and then **the same finish** only, even while you are running around. You could think of all the other things and then look uncoordinated, like trying to walk using four or five crutches at the same time. You'll end up with the ball getting by you or hitting you on the head.*

__DRILL #2:__ When you are comfortably hitting every ball over the net and into the court, have your friend vary slightly the height and speed of his toss. By now you may move back, closer to the service line.

Have your friend toss some higher balls, too. As much as possible, let the ball slow down and come to a comfortable height by staying away from the bounce. Let the ball curve fully after the bounce, up and then down below the waist level, where it is most comfortable to hit with a lift.

If this is not possible, it is because your friend is tossing the balls too fast or too close to you. Have him adjust his toss to a gentle one, a little to your right side. At this stage your friend needs to make things easy for you, not difficult. You want to learn to find the ball and to work out how close to the ball you would start the acceleration of your hand and racket. You want to learn control for the rest of your life, rather than going for speed and power first.

Taking the racket back to get more power is also called the backswing. It is something developed personally, by yourself, without even thinking about it. No one should try to help you by telling you to take your racket back or showing the backswing to you. You'll develop it gradually and naturally, when you start increasing the power in your shots.

Be economical in your moves, slow and deliberate in your swing. If you do a lot of fast moving at these low speeds it may trap you later. Can you imagine how much faster you would have to move at the higher speeds? If you rush on a slow ball, you'll probably panic on a fast ball. Practice the other way around, doing things as slowly as you can. Once you groove-in a slow motion for a slow ball, you'll do things instinctively faster for a faster ball.

The more you wait and keep your cool in these learning stages, the better you'll learn to use your time.

Work out your own timing, depending on the speed of the ball coming to you. Wait until well after the bounce before swinging. Don't let anyone rush you. Many people like to help by urging you to prepare or to swing. This will only interfere with your own computations. You need to work this out by yourself, from your own viewpoint.

You will definitely notice if you are late in your swing. You have all the data now, and the quieter the world around you, the better you can do.

The best help you can get from your friend is gentle advice, "wait for the ball," or "don't rush."

Pretty soon you'll start getting the feel that you are accelerating from the ball on. If you get your racket close to the ball before you accelerate, you will have control. If you rush your stroke and strike too early, the ball may come out too hard and without control. That is why I say **touch** *the ball, or* **push** *it. When you push something, you touch it before you put your force to it.*

In tennis this is done by accurately finding the ball, then accelerating from very close to the contact point on. You can develop this feel easily. Just feel that you touch the ball before you hit. Slowly you'll realize how soon you can accelerate without losing your control, and you'll develop a stronger and stronger **push.**

Waiting for the right moment to swing is probably the most delicate part of the game. Almost every human being tends to overreact. Over 80 percent of the mistakes made by professional tennis players are caused by starting the swing too early, rather than late.

A word of caution here. Starting to swing too early, then slowing down at mid-swing (sometimes unconsciously) to compensate, and accelerating again, feels like a late swing, when, in reality, it was too early a start.

Leave your right hand touching your left shoulder at the end of your swing, until you see where the ball has gone. After that bring it back to your bellybutton. By doing this you create a relationship between the end of your swing and your placement.

That is the only mental image of "position" that you need to keep, where your right hand and arm are at the finish of the stroke. This will help you complete your stroke 99.9 percent of the time, no matter what is happening to your body and balance, or how difficult the situation may be. Just like the pros, you'll never forget to finish your swing.

DRILL #3: Slowly you'll start noticing that the height and direction of your shot depend only on the angle of your racket. The swing feels the same all the time. It ends the same whether the ball is lower, higher, further away, or closer to you.

If you angle your racket slightly to your right when you touch the ball, the ball will go to your right. If you angle your racket to your left, the ball will go there, as shown in the following diagrams:

(seen from above)

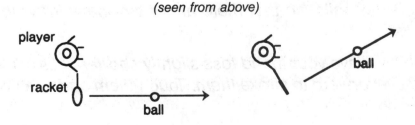

Practice this in the drill. Aim some balls to the center, some to your right, and some to your left, taking care not to hit your friend.

In both instances you would continue the swing toward your left shoulder, finishing the same.

DRILL #4: If you open the racket face, the ball will go higher up. If you close the racket face, the ball will go lower over the net, as shown in the following diagrams:

This closing or opening of the racket is done with a little turn of the forearm prior to the swing and kept throughout. The grip always stays the same. Lifting your elbow will also close the racket face.

Practice this. Hit some higher balls and some lower ones by slightly varying the opening of the racket, without disturbing the path of your stroke.

Note

If your friend is a well-coordinated, athletic person, and you succeed in hitting the ball gently in his direction, he can catch it and keep tossing you the same ball over and over. This is particularly good when you only have a few balls. Otherwise you must have a good supply of balls, so that there aren't too many interruptions to these drills.

DRILL #5: Have your friend toss slightly shorter balls, so that you have to move forward to stroke them. Touch them and touch your left *shoulder again. This is your swing, whether you are on the move or stationary. You can add momentum to it when you wish by slightly increasing the movement before the impact. Just be careful not to disturb the racket angle very much.*

*   **DRILL #6:** *Start from the left sideline, a few feet in front of the service line. Turn to your right, and start to walk parallel to the net, as shown below. (Young children should be much closer to the net, according to their build, age, and coordination.)*

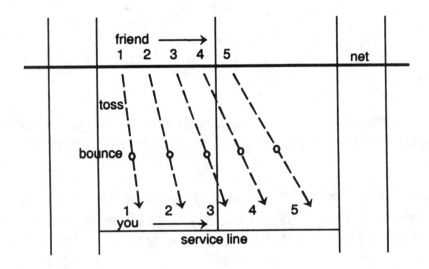

*   *Have your friend toss the ball a little in front of you so that you'll hit it while walking forward. You don't need to stop to hit it. Walk very naturally, as if you were going down the street, all the way to the right sideline, hitting four or five balls in between. Your friend also walks across the court, a little behind you, on his side of the net, leaving an open court for you to hit to.*

*   **DRILL #7:** *When you get used to hitting balls while walking forward, hit forehands while walking backwards, from the right sideline to the left one, as shown in the next diagram. Your friend can toss the ball close to you so that you have to move back before hitting each ball. This will teach you to put some distance between you and the ball when it is coming too close or right at you.*

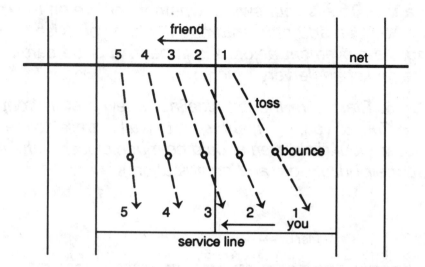

You can actually combine these last two drills, hitting four or five balls while walking forward, then four or five balls while walking backwards.

You will also learn to walk slower or faster to find the ball. It will all depend on the speed and placement of your friend's toss, and the place where you want to meet the ball. It is always like catching the ball, whether you have to run to get it or not. Always find it first, and again, don't rush the stroke.

DRILL #8: Put a can of balls in the center of the court, a few feet in front of the service line. Stand right in front of the can. Your friend tosses a ball to your right side, a few feet from you. Get to it and hit it. Turn to your left and come back to the center. Round the can from the backcourt, turning to your right, while your friend tosses another ball to your right. Get to it and hit it, get back to the center, rounding the can again, and so on (diagram).

This will teach you "pivoting," that is, turning to go in one direction, then turning to go in another direction. Always walk or run forward in this drill, not sideways or backward. Do this naturally, turning and turning again.

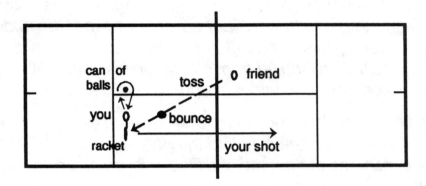

Don't turn your back toward your friend or to the net at any time during this drill. You must always go around the can from behind. This way you can see your opponent's court at all times.

Synchronizing the body to the strokes is really an instinctive process that you develop with the drills in this book. Sometimes you'll need to hurry, just like when the pedestrian light starts blinking and the traffic begins roaring to a start. But the more naturally you walk, as if you were walking down the street or window shopping, the better you'll learn to play.

The tennis court is quite small, three or four steps to each side, a few more forward. But you can't lose time preparing your shot before you get somewhere near the ball. Many people start their swing before they run. They lose valuable time that could be used to get to the ball.

The shot preparation occurs when you are getting near the ball, or the ball is getting near you. With practice you can get to the stage where your arms feel independent of your body position or movement. You'll be able to find the ball smoothly and move through the swing whether you are on the run, falling forward or backward, or completely stationary and facing the net.

Now, as you progress, move the can a little farther from the net. Have your friend toss the ball farther away, slowly increasing the difficulty of the drill.

Always be in control of what you are doing. You may have to do some running to get to the ball, but go slowly toward the middle and make sure your friend doesn't toss the next ball too soon. He shouldn't toss the ball too far from you or too fast either. At this stage of your development it would ruin your swing.

If it starts to go bad, go back to an easier part of the drill. The criteria here is that you have to find the ball well and finish the stroke properly. Otherwise the degree of difficulty is too steep and you need to go either to a slower toss or a ball closer to your reach, or both.

DRILL #9: After you have completed Drill #8 forty or fifty times and you feel you have gotten your stroke grooved-in, you can have your friend feed the ball with a tennis racket. He should do this only if he can control the ball with the racket. (By now, you may move well behind the service line.)

While doing the drill, run gently to the side where the ball is coming. The ball bounces. Slow down and wait. Find the ball gently, with little momentum in your swing. Accelerate the arm at contact, bending it farther when you touch the ball. Finish with the right hand touching your left shoulder. Leave the hand there while you turn toward the middle of the court, seeing where you placed the ball in your opponent's court. Bring the racket down gently into the left hand. Center the racket near your bellybutton, while slowly going to the center of the court. Round the can, and so on, over and over.

You can alternate with your friend, and feed balls to him. Trade places with him. Bounce the ball a little to your front and to your right. Using the same gentle swing as in your drills, direct the ball as if you were tossing it to your friend, so that he can hit it comfortably.

*DRILL #10: As soon as you feel in complete control of your stroke and the ball, you can get rid of the can. Stand midway between the service line and the baseline, or perhaps closer to the service line, whichever is to your liking. Now you can hit balls back and forth with someone good enough, **with your forehand only** (or forehand to forehand if your friend is also at this stage).*

*Hit at a slow pace, a few feet over the net. **Always return,** at least a few feet, toward the center after each hit. Pivot back and forth, just like in the drill around the can.*

When you are able to hit ten or twenty balls back and forth, move further back. Work out the speed gradually to a medium-paced rally.

You'll find that there is plenty of time between each of your hits. At this pace the ball takes between one and a half to two seconds to go from baseline to baseline, assuming that it cleared the net by a few feet and that it bounced near the service line. Therefore, the ball can take from three to four seconds between the time you strike it until it comes back into your racket again.

The topspin forehand

That is plenty of time for you to follow through all the way in your swing, to take a few steps toward the middle, to turn again and go back to hit another forehand.

You can do everything as you did during the drills, without rushing at all. On the contrary, emphasize waiting and moving slowly. Find the ball well and finish your stroke all the way.

Choose whatever feels best, is the least strenuous, and allows you to stay loose. Swing smoothly and firmly, without disturbing the feel of lifting the ball and completing your swing. All the small adjustments to the flight of the ball, body motion and position, distance, etc., will start to occur instinctively. They will all build automatically if you keep your focus on finding the ball and finishing your stroke.

Drifting to the Center

There is usually a four-inch line at the center of the baseline to indicate the center of the court. While playing a match, or hitting back and forth, you don't need to get to the middle of the court all the time. After striking the ball, drift slowly toward the middle. Then if you see your opponent hit the ball behind you (the place you just left), turn right back to get the ball.

As you watch a professional match, you may see that players sometimes skip sideways toward the center, usually after they hit a crosscourt shot. They are just staying in the vicinity of their opponent's highest percentage shot, which would be another crosscourt. If there is any kind of pressure, or they need to get somewhere fast, they pivot for their run.

This pivoting is common to many sports and a very natural thing to do. You see kids of a very tender age turning in whichever direction they want to go. As a matter of fact, they do that before they learn to walk.

In order for you to learn to play naturally and efficiently, even under pressure, you need to groove-in your pivoting from the start. The drill with the can of balls is the best way to get used to it. From my experience with students, learning to sidestep at this stage just impairs coordination and timing and severely complicates the whole learning process. (More on this subject in Chapter Two on "Misconceptions.")

Errors

The most common error is to rush arm movement, which destroys your feel of the ball. Sometimes it pays to wait too long when you are learning or practicing, because this way you'll find out exactly how long you can wait. If you get used to rushing, you'll never know how long you could have waited before swinging. The compensations players create to make up for being early usually hide the perception of this error. The difference may be in the one hundredths of a second, but it will affect your play.

Focusing Your Attention

Introducing additions to the techniques, like worrying about your steps, your body position, and the like, may complicate your learning process. There is a difference between focusing your attention and just being aware of something while focusing on something else.

Good concentration is focusing all your attention into one thing. The more you isolate that particular thing from the rest, the better your concentration is.

Human beings tend to lose their concentration easily. Top pros don't. Not all pros act the same between points, but, while the ball is in play, there is nothing else in the world to the pro but finding it and getting it back.

Of course, they are aware of other things. But, again, their focus is directed toward the feel of a very few important things that are clearly explained in this book.

Students who have their whole attention on the feel of the ball and the finish of the swing look very stylish and coordinated. On the other hand, those who pay attention to their feet usually look stiff, unnatural, and sometimes plainly uncoordinated. The reason behind that is that they focus their attention on things that need to happen naturally, taking valuable attention away from the most important thing, which is finding and feeling the ball.

"Racket Back"

A beginner should never be told, as stressed in most conventional teaching techniques, to take the racket back. Taking your racket back early, or hard, or fast, separates your hand from the ball. You won't find the ball well.

There is no early, separate backswing in the greatest strokes in the game. There is simply a movement back and forth where the player is generating momentum according to the power he wants in the shot, while still carefully finding the ball.

In modern forehands this momentum is generated mostly by a turn from the waist up. It is like a twisted spring that will come back with force. The right hand also goes back and forth just prior to the hit, but the player feels that the hand is still near the ball, therefore *finding it* well before exploding from the ball forward.

If you are a beginner, let it be a gentle, slow movement at first. Keep in mind that you are learning control first, before you hit as hard as a pro. You want to find the ball perfectly and smoothly and to feel the impact as long as you can.

Your backswing may be circular or straight down and up. It may be almost nonexistent at first. As long as you find the ball well and you don't disturb your racket angle, there isn't much difference between the two. This part of the swing is peculiar to each player and shouldn't be disturbed. It is the way they "find" the ball.

Hitting High

Do not fear hitting high over the net. Many people have the idea that they need to hit down to get the ball to drop in the court. From baseline to baseline the distance is 78 feet. Your slow backcourt groundstroke has a mathematical and physical impossibility of clearing your opponent's baseline, no matter how high you hit the ball, unless it is carried by the wind. The same goes for a medium-speed shot hit with plenty of topspin.

One very common error is to hit the ball very low over the net. This causes more errors than hitting safely over the net. I remember a stage in my life when I lost more matches to the net than to my opponents.

While practicing groundstrokes, put a string two or three feet above the net and hit over it. Many pros follow this rule, especially the topspin players, who get depth in their shots either by hitting very hard or hitting high over the net, or both.

"Breaking" the Wrist

Do not snap your wrist forward as you hit. It causes you to lose control and possibly strain your arm. Bending the wrist forward is usually a compensation for hitting too early. The player is swinging and the ball isn't quite there yet. He looks for it with the tip of the racket, and the ball often ends up crosscourt.

It is your hand that moves, not just the racket. The racket head is actually slightly behind the hand when you are finding the ball. For a topspin forehand, you should actually be able to see the back of your hand throughout the whole shot.

Forearm Rotation

Forearm rotation helps to lift the ball and rotate it with topspin. The following picture sequence shows this forearm rotation.

Dropping the Racket Head

You can let the racket head drop as low as you like below your hand and below the ball before you hit. This will help you to lift the ball and put topspin to it. Keeping the head of the racket up all the time, as recommended by many tennis teachers, will not only stiffen your swing but also strain your forearm. It is one of the primary causes of "tennis elbow," a chronic pain at the outside of the elbow.

Lifting the Body

Your body will usually help to lift the ball by pulling up. This is a very natural thing to do. The more topspin you hit, the more your body needs to help the lift. To stay low throughout the shot can dampen your feel of lifting and stand in the way of developing a great topspin stroke.

Backing Up

To handle topspin balls coming at you, you may need to move back to get away from the bounce. This way you let the ball lose some of its sting and come to a comfortable height where you can also hit it back with topspin. The most comfortable height to hit a groundstroke with topspin is usually between knee level and waist level.

Attacking a high topspin ball is delicate and risky. The best place to attack such a ball, other than to volley it before it bounces, is to hit it right after the bounce, with the ball at knee level or below. This takes great timing and touch (perfect contact between racket and ball) while the ball is still going fast. It is best to leave that until you are very experienced in the game. During your early tennis development stages, use the safest and most consistent option, which is to let the ball slow down by moving back. Let it come down comfortably, and hit topspin back.

Low Topspin

Not all topspin shots are high. You'll see the pros hitting hard topspin shots low over the net for sharp crosscourts or forceful passing shots.

On a topspin crosscourt shot you can achieve a greater angle than with a flat stroke without having to slow down your shot.

On a topspin passing shot, your opponent has more difficulty handling your ball because it drops much more quickly after crossing the net. (A passing shot is the shot that you hit with a groundstroke to pass an opponent who has come to the net and wants to volley your next shot.)

There are so many advantages to topspin on groundstrokes that they are still being discovered by many of the top pros.

8

The Two-Handed Backhand

When the ball comes to your left side, you have a choice of hitting your backhand with both hands on the grip, or with just one hand on the racket.

Many adults choose a one-handed backhand because their right side is so strong that they prefer to do everything with that side. For children, the two-handed backhand is easier to learn. The two-handed support gives them more strength and it doesn't require a grip change.

A two-handed backhand gives more power and also works out the left side of the body, making for a more balanced physical development overall. The only disadvantage is a slight reduction in reach compared with the one-handed backhand.

A few players have both backhands. They hit topspin two-handed, while they slice with a one-handed shot.

This chapter will teach you the two-handed backhand. The one-handed backhand is explained in the next chapter, and the backhand slice in Chapter Fifteen, "Special Shots."

If you have already decided to hit your backhand one-handed you may skip this chapter and go directly to the next chapter.

The Two-Handed Backhand

Many professionals use this shot, which is really a two-handed forehand from the left side. The palm of the left hand does the driv-

ing, with the right hand just accompanying the process, without interfering with the left hand.

A few pros play a mixture of a two-handed and a one-handed backhand, in which the left hand lets go of the racket at the impact time or right after.

This chapter will teach you the backhand in which you keep both hands on the racket throughout.

The backhand is easier to learn at this stage because by now you have plenty of experience as to how the ball bounces and behaves. You also know how to find the ball before swinging.

In the waiting position, a player with a two-handed backhand keeps his hands closer together than the player with a one-handed backhand, as shown on page 90.

*Keep both hands on the grip, near your bellybutton, while waiting in between shots. Get to the ball, find it well, and follow through over your right shoulder. It is like a mirror copy of your forehand shot, except that you don't release the other hand from the racket. (You can do a few two-handed backhands in front of a mirror. Let the **right** hand go sometimes. You'll see how it resembles your forehand.)*

***DRILL #1:** Go on the court without a racket and stand facing the net six to eight feet in front of the service line. Have your friend toss the ball toward your left side. Let the ball bounce, find it with the palm of your left hand, and push it over the net. Finish with the index finger of your left hand touching your right shoulder. (If you have any difficulty finding the ball, do all the coordination drills of Chapter Five with your **left** hand.)*

Do this drill until you are getting the ball over the net comfortably.

***DRILL #2:** Grab your racket with both hands, as described earlier. Center your hands by your bellybutton, while standing in front of the service line facing the net. (You may "choke up" on the racket as much as you like.) Have your friend toss the ball gently toward your left side. Wait until after the bounce, find the ball well with the center* *of your racket strings, and push it up over the net, bringing both hands over your right shoulder, as shown in the pictures below.*

Repeat this drill thirty or forty times. Get used to keeping your hands near your waist while waiting for the ball, then adjust to the ball as needed. Find the ball mostly with your left hand, and follow through over the right shoulder, leaving the racket there for a split second, while looking where your shot has gone.

The following drills are similar to the ones you did while learning the forehand.

DRILL #3: Your friend tosses short balls toward your backhand side. Get to the ball and hit it gently over the net.

DRILL #4: Hit backhands while walking forward, close to the service line, all the way from the right sideline to the left sideline.

DRILL #5: Hit backhands while walking backward, all the way from the left sideline to the right sideline.

DRILL #6: Put the can of balls in the center of the court. Go around the can and to your left, as shown in the diagram on the next page.

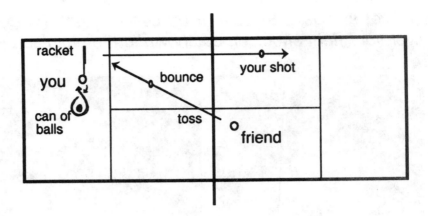

Your friend tosses the ball in front of you. Let the ball bounce, find it with the racket, and lift it over the net, following through over your right shoulder. Turn right immediately and go back to the can, rounding it from the backcourt and turning to your left.

When you begin walking toward the left side of the court, your friend tosses another ball. Get there and hit another backhand, then return to the can of balls and so on.

Never turn your back to your opponent in your turns or after the hit. Turn to your right after your shot, to your left when you round the can.

Swing slowly at first, always in control. Leave the racket at the finish position while you turn toward the center of the court, building up the relationship between the finish of your stroke and the placement of the ball in your opponent's court.

The racket face angle will determine the height and direction of your shot. After a while the stroke will become quite automatic, going from the ball to the shoulder, whether the ball is high or low, close to you or farther away.

It is important that you learn not to slap at the ball, suddenly changing the angle of your wrists. On the contrary, move your hands smoothly through the stroke, feeling the lift you are giving to the ball.

Preferably, the ball should have a forward roll after leaving your racket.

When hitting comfortably from near the service line, move the can farther away from the net a few feet at a time. Have your friend toss the ball slightly farther each time.

Always step up the difficulty of the drill very slowly, so as not to lose the feel of the ball and the finish of the stroke.

DRILL #7: *Same as Drill #6, except that your friend feeds the ball with a tennis racket, but only if he can do it with control and without disrupting your own control.*

DRILL #8: *Get rid of the can. Now you can work out your shots to a medium pace and start brushing up on the ball, the same as you did with your forehand, to give the ball more of a forward roll (topspin).*

Dropping the racket head below the ball and lifting it up over your shoulder will increase your topspin. You'll be able to clear the net at a good height and still get the ball in the court, even when you hit hard.

The two-handed topspin backhand

DRILL #9: *When you are satisfied with your progress and are confidently hitting your backhand without a miss, you can start a one forehand, one backhand routine.*

Walk naturally, first to your right. Your friend feeds a ball to your forehand side. Hit a forehand. Turn to your left. Walk. Your friend tosses a ball to your backhand side. Hit a backhand. Turn to your right, walk, hit a forehand, and so on.

Do this until you are completely comfortable on both sides.

Now your friend can mix up forehands and backhands as he likes, but always giving you enough time in between shots to turn and start to return toward the middle.

DRILL #10: You are ready to hit back and forth. You need to do this with someone who has good control of the ball.

Keep the ball in play at a medium or slow pace that allows you to find the ball easily and to get it back to the other player with a full and controlled stroke.

Control

I say a controlled stroke because that is the emphasis when learning with this method. You'll very quickly see the relationship between your swing and the ball's velocity and placement.

You can experiment, but be careful not to stray very far from the essence of this technique. Should you make wild strokes, or the other player feed or return the ball wildly, it can severely damage both your swing and confidence.

Confidence

Confidence is built by hitting the same shot over and over a few hundred times. You get to know that you caused it with a specific movement, a specific technique.

Trial and error as a learning method doesn't work well in tennis. There are a million ways to strike the ball, but very, very few of them are really effective.

With the type of stroke I am teaching you, topspin is an easy thing to develop both for the forehand and the backhand. If you can hit topspin consistently from the backcourt, at a medium pace, three to six feet over the net, you are on the way to becoming a good player.

In following junior tennis at the world-ranking level for many years, I have seen that the great majority of top players in the last fifteen years are those who had plenty of topspin in at least one of their strokes in their developing years.

Although topspin has been widely accepted by the best players, most of the various teaching techniques seem to avoid it altogether.

On the contrary, I encourage you to use it right from the beginning. I like to provide students with the best equipment for their stroke, to teach them to play like a pro, to be as consistent as a pro.

You may be using topspin defensively to start with, but sooner or later you'll learn powerful offensive shots that will need a lot of topspin to stay in the court.

I purposely took away the power in the early learning stages with my teaching methods. You focused on feel and control. Now the power will gradually come into your game.

As you gain confidence you'll stroke harder. With a lot of topspin, you can hit as hard as you like. As long as the ball keeps clearing the net and going into the opposite court, this process shouldn't be disturbed.

9

The One-Handed Backhand

This chapter will teach you both the flat and the topspin one-handed backhand.

If you have decided to hit your backhand two-handed, you don't need to go through this chapter at all. Skip it and go directly to Chapter Ten, "The Serve."

The one-handed backhand could be likened to hitting the ball with the back of the hand, as shown in the photograph below.

[CAUTION: Don't try this because it hurts the hand.]

To learn this backhand quickly, put the thumb of your right hand against the throat of the racket, as shown in the photograph below.

DRILL #1: *Stand about eight to ten feet from the net. Have your friend stand on the other side of the net, tossing easy balls toward your left side. Meet the ball well in front of you (Picture 1) and gently push it up and over the net, toward the open court. Finish with your arm fully extended and up (Picture 2).*

1

2

This is an upward effort, both to lift the ball and the arm.

Don't resort to hitting the ball hard to get it over the net. Just push the ball upward more than forward, sending it a few feet above the net.

After a few shots turn slightly to your left. See if this helps your swing.

Leave the arm up at the finish for a couple of seconds to build the relationship between your finish and the placement of your shot in your opponent's court.

If you have good control of the ball, you can hit it slowly toward your friend, who will catch it and toss it to you again.

The following drills are similar to the ones you did while learning the forehand.

DRILL #2: Have your friend toss some shorter balls. Move up to the ball, find it, and hit it gently, up and over the net.

DRILL #3: Hit several backhands while walking from your right sideline to the left sideline, with your friend tossing the ball short and a bit to your front. Meet the ball toward the right side of your body, as in Picture 1, and extend your arm upward in the direction of your opponent's court, as in Picture 2.

DRILL #4: Hit backhands while walking backward, from the left sideline to the right sideline. Your friend tosses the ball in your direction so that you have to move back to hit. Keep the right arm up at the end of your swing for a short while, as in the prior drills. Your friend shouldn't rush you by feeding the next ball too soon.

You could also do a combination of these last two drills, hitting four or five backhands while walking forward, and four or five backhands while walking backward.

As you gain confidence in your shots, gradually start moving your hand toward the grip of the racket (Picture 3 on page 126). Your left hand will help you support the racket prior to your swing (Picture 4).

3

4

You don't need to move your right hand all the way onto the racket handle early in your development. Keep your hand wherever it feels comfortable.

If you feel confident that you are ready and are finding the ball well, you can place your right hand on the grip, but keep the angle between the racket and your arm close to perpendicular, as in Picture 2. Otherwise you'll get used to "breaking" your wrist, following through with your racket only, instead of fully extending the arm.

DRILL #5: *Put the can of balls in the center of the court, near the service line or slightly in front of the service line. Round the can to your left, as shown in the diagram, looking at your friend who is ready to toss you a ball toward your backhand side.*

Turn to your left and start walking toward the left side of your court.

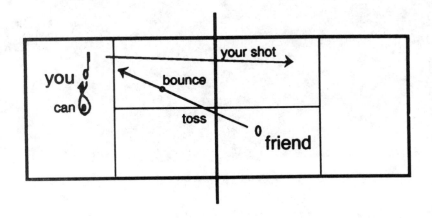

Your friend tosses the ball slightly in front of you, making sure it bounces well before it gets to you. Get near the ball, finding it toward the right side of your body, your right arm fully extended. As you touch the ball, accelerate your arm upward and lift the ball over the net.

You end up with your right arm fully extended toward the net, while your left arm extends backward to keep your balance.

After finishing your swing, turn to your right, with the arm still up. When you finish your turn, bring the racket back to both hands, while walking back toward the center of the court. Round the can again and repeat the process over and over.

Don't turn your back toward your opponent's court. After you hit, turn to your right. Round the can turning to your left.

The end of the swing

In this drill it is best to use the backhand grip all the time in order to get used to it. Small changes and adjustments will occur, both in your grip and your swing. This is okay, because you are developing a better feel and the most efficient swing possible.

As long as you are clearing the net safely and have the ball speed under control, keep lifting away.

Gradually move away from the net and toward the backcourt, continuing this drill from farther back.

You can leave your thumb against the backside of the grip, as shown in Picture 5, or you can drop it all the way around it, as shown in Picture 6. As players get very good, they usually end up with the thumb down and around the grip.

5

6

Topspin

The flat and the topspin one-handed backhands are similar. Top-spin will be a natural consequence of your lift.

Ideally, your ball should be rotating with topspin from an early stage in your learning.

It is easier to muscle the ball with topspin using your forehand. To develop the same strong feel in your backhand you'll need to practice until you develop your back and shoulder muscles.

Just keep pulling up your swing, brushing up on the ball. Start with the racket head below the ball and pull it upward toward the sky.

Do it gently, slowly building up your strength. Do not use much force. Get feel and control first.

***DRILL #6:** After you have excellent control and get every ball over the net and in the court, get rid of the can of balls.*

Go onto the center of the court, behind the service line, with your racket in the normal waiting position. Have your friend feed a ball to your forehand side. Get to the ball and hit a forehand. Turn to your left. Change to your backhand grip. Pointing the butt of the racket toward the ball in your friend's hand will help this process.

Your friend then feeds a ball to your backhand side, close to your reach. Get to it and hit a backhand. Leave the racket up while you turn to your right. Then put the racket butt near your bellybutton, changing to your forehand grip.

Your friend now feeds a ball to your forehand side. Get to it and hit a forehand, turn to your left, and so on.

Your left hand can help you get your backhand grip by pulling back from the throat of the racket. At the same time the grip slides inside your right hand, while you set your fingers closer together.

Do not look at your grip while changing from forehand to backhand or vice versa. The grip needs to be felt, not seen.

If you are experiencing any trouble, take a few minutes and practice this grip change with your eyes closed. Face the net with your forehand grip. Turn your shoulders to your left, while pulling back from the racket throat with your left hand and slightly loosening your right hand grip. Point the racket butt to an imaginary ball coming to your backhand side and tighten your right hand grip again. This sequence will change your grip inside your right hand.

After that tighten your arms and shoulders as if you were preparing for a backhand stroke. Then face the net again, centering your forehand grip by your bellybutton.

Do this back and forth until the grip change becomes automatic, together with your turning to your left and to your right.

Some players, including many professionals, bring their shoulders around, right shoulder toward the ball in the backhand, left shoulder toward the ball in the forehand. This is good (it keeps the body moving), as long as you keep finding the ball with your hand, not your shoulder.

DRILL #7: Now your friend can mix up forehands and backhands. He can also slowly step up the difficulty of the drill. Always feel in control, otherwise cut the difficulty back.

Do this drill until you are getting every ball smoothly into your opponent's court.

Rallying

Now you are ready to hit back and forth. You'll need someone to hit with that has good control. Start at a slow pace, keeping the ball in play as long as you can.

This is not a game yet. You are still developing your strokes and you want to keep the same feel of control and finish of your stroke.

If you lose the feel of your swing or you lose your confidence, find the ball well and exaggerate the finish of your swing. It should come right back.

The topspin backhand

Control
(For those who skipped the previous chapter)

Keep the ball in play at a medium or slow pace that allows you to find the ball easily and to get it back to the other player with a full and controlled stroke.

I say a controlled stroke because that is the emphasis when learning with this method. You'll very quickly see the relationship between your swing and the ball's velocity and placement.

You can experiment, but be careful not to stray very far from the essence of this technique. Should you start to make wild strokes, or the other player feed or return the ball wildly, it can severely damage both your swing and your confidence.

Confidence
(For those who skipped the previous chapter)

Confidence is built by hitting the same shot over and over a few hundred times. You get to know that you caused it with a specific movement, a specific technique.

Trial and error as a learning method doesn't work well in tennis. There are a million ways of striking the ball, but very, very few of them are really effective.

With the type of stroke I am teaching you, topspin is an easy thing to develop both for the forehand and the backhand. If you can hit topspin consistently from the backcourt, at a medium pace, three to six feet over the net, you are on the way to becoming a good player.

In following junior tennis at the world-ranking level for many years, I have seen that the great majority of top players in the last fifteen years are those who had plenty of topspin in at least one of their strokes in their developing years.

Although topspin has been widely accepted by the best players, most of the various teaching techniques seem to avoid it altogether.

On the contrary, I encourage you to use it right from the beginning. I like to provide students with the best equipment for their stroke, to teach them to play like a pro, to be as consistent as a pro.

You may be using topspin defensively to start with, but sooner or later you'll learn powerful offensive shots that will need a lot of topspin to stay in the court.

I purposely took away the power in the early learning stages with my teaching methods. You focused on feel and control. Now the power will gradually come into your game.

As you gain confidence you'll stroke harder. With a lot of topspin, you can hit as hard as you like. As long as the ball keeps clearing the net and going into the opposite court, this process shouldn't be disturbed.

Advanced Topspin

Many top players can hit tremendous one-handed topspin backhands from almost any position. Prior to the shot they point the butt of the racket to the incoming ball, lowering the racket below the ball. From there they hit upward, getting plenty of lift and ball rotation, while still hitting the ball very hard.

Depending on the racket face angle, they can achieve—with the same stroke—a low passing shot, a forceful crosscourt, a high and deep looping shot, or a deceiving topspin lob.

It isn't hard to do. It is just a question of being far enough below the ball to create plenty of lift.

10

The Serve

The serve is the first ball hit in every point.

The point continues until someone hits the ball into the net or outside the boundaries of his opponent's court, or is unable to get to the ball before it bounces twice. The player who makes the error loses the point. (Any ball touching the correct boundary line, no matter how slight, is considered to have landed inside the court.)

The Serving Sequence

In a match you must serve from behind the baseline (see drawing of court below). You serve the first point from the right (position 1), hitting the ball to the opposite service court (shaded area 1). Serve the second point from the left (position 2), hitting the ball to the opposite service court (shaded area 2), the third point from the right, and so on.

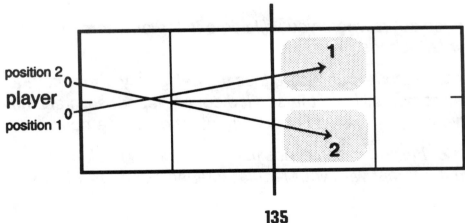

The same player serves an entire game, comprised of several points. Your opponent serves the next game, and so on. One game is part of a set, and one set is part of the entire match. The full scoring system is explained in Chapter Twelve.

A player can retrieve a serve only after it has bounced in the service court.

The Drills

You can learn to serve quickly through a simple procedure. Stand about six feet from the net, slightly to the right of the center line, as shown in the diagram.

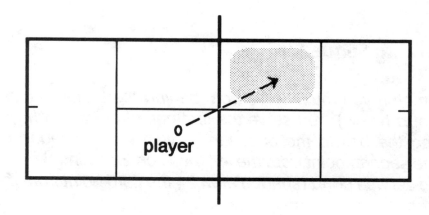

The service court where you will serve is the one across the net and to your left (shaded area).

DRILL #1: Without your racket, toss the ball gently overhead (Picture 1) over the net and into the service court. Repeat several times and observe how the ball curves down into the service court.

DRILL #2: From the same position as in Drill #1, pick up your racket from the throat with your regular forehand grip, as it if were a

1   2

shorter racket. Hold the ball in your left hand, with your hands slightly above your face (Picture 2).

Toss the ball above your racket strings and push it gently with your racket, over the net and into the service court.

This push is done by extending your arm toward your target as shown in the picture on the next page.

Serve balls from this position near the net until you are successful in getting the ball in the proper court. Always advance your hand, rather than just the racket head.

*   **DRILL #3:** *Get a bucketful of balls and do the following: serving as shown, gently hit a serve into the correct service court. Every time you get the ball in the service court, you are allowed one step back toward the baseline, staying to the right of the center (see diagram below).*

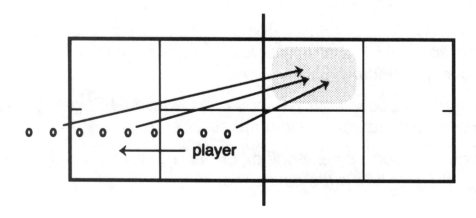

Every time you miss a serve, take a step forward toward the net.

By moving away from the net only after a successful serve, you'll instinctively develop a feel for the serve. You will sense how much power you need to release to get the ball over the net and still drop it into the service court.

If the ball touches the top of the net and lands in the correct service court (this is called a "let"), repeat the serve from the same position.

You can move your hand gradually toward the normal grip position, or you can keep the racket short for a while. Do what you feel is best in order to develop your serve at your own speed.

Stretch your arm upward to get the ball to curve over the net.

The angle of the racket will determine the direction of the ball.

As you get better, move your arm and racket across the ball, from left to right, to give it spin. This will add to your control, and is a significant part of developing a good serve. Just be aware of the racket angle while you move your arm. The more you want to spin the ball, the more you need to angle your racket to the left.

Feel your arm movement, especially the upward push of the ball. As you develop a better serve, exaggerate the length of your push past the impact point. Extend your arm farther and up to get the ball to clear the net, increasing the curve and the spin, rather than going for a hard hit.

When you get to the baseline keep going back one step at a time until you are near the back fence or wall of the court. This will lengthen your swing. You may also be turning to get more power, your toss may be a little higher, your swing longer. Let all this develop as needed to get the ball over the net and into the service court.

CAUTION: *Before you try harder serves, you need to get used to ending your swing with your right arm across your body and to your left, as shown in the next picture sequence. Otherwise you might hit your legs with your racket.*

This is not a problem in the beginning, because your swing is smooth and slow and probably stops with your arm in the net's direction.

As you lengthen your swing and increase your arm speed, first bring your right hand up toward your right to spin the ball (Pictures 1 and 2), then, when your arm starts falling, bring your hand toward your left hip, finishing with the racket throat in your left hand, as shown in Picture 3.

1   2   3

DRILL #4: *As soon as you can serve consistently from the back-court go behind the baseline and start serving from there, still positioned slightly to the right of the center line.*

You are not allowed to touch the baseline or the inside of the court as you serve (this is called a "foot fault"). Your foot can land inside the court only after the ball leaves your racket.

Serve ten to twenty balls into the correct service court.

***DRILL #5:** Come close to the net again, standing to the left of the center line. Now you'll be serving to the service court across the net and to your right. Repeat the same process that you did on the right side of your court: one step back for every ball you get in and one step forward for every ball you miss.*

Continue past the baseline, then come back just behind the baseline, to the left of center, and serve ten to twenty balls into the service court from there.

***DRILL #6:** Practice a few balls from the right side, then a few from the left side. As soon as you feel good about getting the ball where you want, alternate, serving one ball from the right side, one from the left, and so on. Work until your accuracy is well over 50 percent.*

***DRILL #7:** In a match you are allowed two serves, that is, two chances to get your serve in. If you miss your first serve, you then take a second serve. You better get this one in, otherwise you lose the point. Missing both the first and second serves is called a "double fault," and the point goes to your opponent.*

"Let" balls (touching the net and bouncing into the service court) have to be repeated from the same position, whether it is a first or a second serve.

Now practice this way: Serve one ball from the right side. If you get it in the correct service court, count it as your point, then serve from the left side. If you missed that first serve, go for your second one. If you make it good, count it as your point. Otherwise count it as your opponent's point.

Now serve from the left side, using the same procedure: first serve, second serve if necessary, either your point or your opponent's point.

Alternate serving from the right and the left up to ten or twenty points or until you no longer serve any double faults. Double faults should be a rare thing, even at this stage.

After that, switch to your opponent's court and serve ten or twenty points from there.

This is the basic learning process for your serve. You can do all this by yourself. Many professionals go out on the court with a bucket of balls and practice dozens of serves. You can do the same, both to learn and to develop your serve, but only after you have gradually developed your arm and shoulder muscles.

If you don't have many balls to do these drills, serve gently and have a friend catch your serves on the other side. He can then send the ball back to you after each serve.

As soon as you have completed these drills successfully, turn to the next chapter, "The Rally Game," to improve upon your skills and get ready for a game.

Later in your development you can lengthen your swing by going down and then up with your arms, prior to the swing, like the pros, but to do it here in the beginning may complicate your progress.

You now have an easy and effective way of serving with which you can start the point and play with anyone. A gradual development of your skills with many hours of practice is much more efficient than learning too many things at the start. Get on the court and practice what you already know, before tackling the advanced player's full-motion serve.

Advanced Serves

The professionals get momentum on the serve with a very coordinated motion similar to an overhead pitch.

The racket starts in front, resting in both hands. The arms separate, going slightly down, then up, while the player leans forward, turns the shoulders, and arches the back. The left hand releases the ball in an upward toss, coordinated with the upward movement of the right arm. The right arm bends, looping the racket behind the back. The player feels the accumulating momentum (power). The arm and racket are then thrust forward and upward, while the body uncoils and stretches, leaning into the court and jumping off the ground. The racket makes contact with the ball, moving as far up as possible, and making a circular arch that goes first to the right, then down to the left. The acceleration and stretching go way past the impact point with the ball, while the player falls forward, stepping into the court.

The Slice Serve

In the slice serve (for a right-hander) the ball would spin, as seen from the player's viewpoint, from left to right, as if it were rolling forward on a wall to the player's left. As a result, the ball curves toward the left of the server.

The American Twist Serve

The American Twist serve is similar to hitting topspin in your groundstrokes, except that it is more difficult in the serve to get the ball to roll forward and still clear the net.

Players achieve this serve by tossing the ball slightly behind themselves or to their left, then bringing the ball up and forward with a closed racket face. The ball gets a combination of topspin and some sideways rotation, curving down and slightly to the left during flight, but then jumps to the right and up on the bounce, curving again to the left.

This serve is very safe, because the ball drops very quickly. You can clear the net by as much as three to four feet.

Top players use it for second serves, not only for its safety, but also for its effectiveness in keeping the opponent from attacking the serve due to its kick.

For the serve-and-volley player, this serve's slower flight speed gives them plenty of time to get to the net, while making it difficult for their opponent to drive through for a forceful return.

Contrary to the flat serve and the slice, the American Twist hangs in the air much longer, then accelerates on the way down to the bounce, regaining speed, and kicking way up. This particular feature makes it more difficult to judge. Returning players have to resort to moving back to return this serve with a full drive or making a slower and safer return.

The American Twist serve

Professionals use different degrees of spin according to the surface and the score situation. Most first serves have some spin.

Only on grass does the American Twist lose some of its efficiency. The ball slides and doesn't grab the surface on the bounce, losing the characteristic high kick that otherwise makes it so difficult to return.

Summing up, spinning the ball in your serve creates curves that help get the ball in the service box. It allows the player to hit the serve much harder with a smaller percentage of errors.

It isn't a difficult stroke to learn, except that you have to hit up much more than you ever imagined. The best way to learn it is to exaggerate both the upward pull and the spin.

11

The Rally Game

Now that you can serve and have good control of your forehand and backhand strokes, you are ready for a game from the back-court.

To improve your skills and enjoy yourself, play a **"Rally Game."** The object is to hit as many balls as possible over the net and into the court, without trying to finish the point. Just return the ball to your opponent so he or she can return it to you.

This game is played from the backcourt, with each player letting the ball bounce before hitting it. It will teach you to keep the ball in play until you can hit back and forth at a medium pace. The other player should do the same, striving for control, getting as many balls as possible back to you.

It is not unusual at this stage to see thirty or forty consecutive balls going back and forth in each rally.

Start with an easy serve, then keep the ball in play, always returning it close to your friend's reach.

The player missing a shot or hitting beyond their opponent's reach counts it as losing the point. The same applies for hard or forceful shots. The emphasis is on keeping the ball in play where the opponent can get to it comfortably.

Even professionals hit like that in many practice sessions, or when they warm up prior to the start of a match.

Keeping Score

One player serves until one of the players gets to ten points. Count that as one game. Then the other player serves to ten points, and so on.

This training will help you become consistent, which is the basis of any match play.

The Ideal Partner

In choosing the partner you hit with, get someone who wants to commit to playing safely.

If either you or your friend think that playing tennis is hitting all winners, change your mind for this Rally Game. Take it as playing the piano, not banging it, or like dancing without stepping on your partner's feet. Neither of you wants to embarrass yourself or each other, so enjoy playing back and forth with control.

Your body may need to build up to match your skills. Practicing as shown, with long ball exchanges, will build up your strength, your resistance, and your patience.

Be efficient. Don't exert too much effort and try to kill the ball. Efficiency is the ratio of effort to the result you get. The less effort overall and the smoother the swing, the better off you'll be when learning to play. You'll end up feeling the ball much better and having plenty of control over your shots.

As you progress, you can speed up your shots gradually. You'll play more topspin, stronger games, stronger opponents. You have all the data now for the backcourt game and you need only to practice to improve your game.

At this stage I usually send people to play, without any theory lessons of any kind, for several months. If they want to play with me, I *usually string a rope across the net, about three feet above it, and we hit back and forth, or do special drills. (See Chapter Sixteen on "Drills for Development.")*

I recommend that you become a proficient backcourt player before you learn to play the net game. Being close to the net gives the player a totally different view of the opponent's court, as shown in the following pictures, both taken at eye level.

Standing near the net

From the baseline, you see the other court through the net (unless you are more than six feet tall).

Near the net, you see the other court from above the net. This latter view will give you the impression that you need to hit down to get the ball in the court, which is true for the volleys and smash.

But it is very important to get used to hitting up on the groundstrokes first and to control the height of your shot with your racket angle, not by hitting down.

This is why small children usually learn their groundstrokes so easily and so well. They see the net as a high obstacle and they hit up. Later on, as they grow up and gain power, they keep the same stroke pattern and start closing the racket face to keep the ball in the court, rather than hitting down on the ball.

You can do the same by staying in the backcourt and using topspin until you get very proficient in the Rally Game.

After that read Chapter Fourteen, "Volley and Smash."

12

The Scoring System

In tennis there is a peculiar way of counting points. Adopted in the last century, tennis scoring has been kept almost unchanged because it gives matches a special flavor.

This scoring balances the game in such a way that you always have a chance at winning, even if you have lost every point, until the match is over.

The only significant change in this century has been the implementation of a tiebreaker to avoid marathons and make the game more suitable for TV broadcasting.

The match is divided into segments, called sets. Usually a maximum of three sets are played in a tournament match, while major championships require five sets for men.

Sets are divided into games.

Players alternate serving one game each until one reaches six games, which gives him one set. Sets must be won by a margin of two games. The score can be 6–0, 6–1, 6–2, 6–3, or 6–4. If the score reaches 5–5 (also called 5–all), it has to be won 7–5. If the score reaches 6–6 (6–all), then the special tiebreaker game will be played and the set will end at 7–6.

If you see a 7–6 result for a set you know the players were tied at six games each and a tiebreaker was played.

Winning a three-set match requires winning 2 sets to 1. The result is either 2 sets to 0 (zero is called "love" in tennis), or if each player wins one of the first two sets, they then play a third and deciding set, and one player will win by a score of 2 sets to 1. This last set is called the "final set."

In the best-of-five-set matches, a player must win three sets. Therefore, the score is either 3 sets to 0, 3 sets to 1, or 3 sets to 2. Some of these best-of-five-set matches are very long, lasting four or five hours. Usually a three-set match goes from one hour, for the easier matches, to two or two-and-a-half hours.

When a match is started, players first "spin" a tennis racket or toss a coin to decide who will serve first and which side of the court they will be on for the first game. The winner of the toss has the choice of his preference on one of those decisions. If you decide to serve or return, then your opponent has the choice of side. If you choose the side, then your opponent has the choice of serving or of returning your serve.

Change of side is required after one game, three games, five games, and so on (an odd sum of games) in each set. Most courts are built approximately north-south lengthwise, and the sun angle varies according to the time of the day. The sun's position will affect players more on one side than the other. Players usually choose the better side for their own first service game.

When you win the toss you also have the right to tell your opponent to choose first. This can be advantageous when a right-hander is playing a left-hander outdoors. The sun's position will affect one player more than the other on one side, both for serving and for high balls. If you win the toss, have your opponent choose first. If he chooses to return, you choose your good side to serve. If he chooses to serve, let him serve from the side that is bad for him and good for you. By the second game the change of side will have you serving without the sun interfering with your toss. If you break your opponent's serve in the first game, you are off to a good start.

Let's say you won the toss and have decided to serve and let your opponent choose sides. Go to the other side, behind the baseline, with two balls in your left hand or one in your hand and one in your pocket.

You will be serving the first game as follows: From the right side of the court serve the first point to your opponent's service court (crosscourt, to your left, as explained in Chapter Ten). If you miss the first serve you get a second one. If you miss the second one it's a double fault and the point goes to your opponent.

Whoever wins the first point gets the score of 15. The server's points are called first. Therefore, it can be either 15–0 (15–love) if you won the point, or 0–15 (love–15) if you lost the point.

Now you serve from the left side. If the score is 15–0 and you win this point, you go to 30–0 (30–love). If you lose this point then it is 15–15 (15–all). If you lost the first two points, then it is 0–30 (love–30).

Continue alternating, serving one point from the right, one from the left, going, for example, from 15–15 to 30–15, then 30–30 (30–all). The next point is called 40. Let's say you win the next point and the score is now 40–30. If you win the following point, you win the game and you are **one-love** in games.

You then change sides of the court and your opponent will serve the next game.

If you get to 40–40 (40–all) it is called "deuce," and deuce games have to be decided by a margin of two points. After 40–40, the next point is called "advantage." It will be either "advantage to the server" (also called "ad-in"), or "advantage to the receiver" ("ad-out"). If the player at advantage wins the next point, he wins the game. If he loses it, the score goes back to deuce, and again, two consecutive points by one player are necessary to win the game. There is no limit to the number of "deuces" that can occur in a game.

Each player serves one game until the set is completed, 6–0 or 6–4 for example, or 7–5. If the score gets to 6–6 (6–all), then the tiebreaker game is played.

The tiebreaker goes as follows: The player whose turn it is to serve will serve the first point from the right, as usual. After the first point his opponent will serve the next two points, the first from his left side, the next one from the right. After that, the serve goes back to the first player, who will serve two points, the first from his left side, the next one from his right.

The serve keeps switching back and forth, with each player serving two points. Those points are counted here one, two, three, four and so on. One player has to get to 7 points to win the tiebreaker and the set, but it has to be by a margin of at least two points.

If the score in points gets tied at 6–6, then the tiebreaker has to be won 8–6. If it goes to 7–7, it has to be won 9–7, and so on. A tiebreaker final score may be 7–0, 7–1, 7–2, 7–3, 7–4, 7–5, 8–6, 9–7, 12–10, 20–18, and the like. There is no limit to the number of points that could be played in a tiebreaker if there is a succession of ties, but the chances of it going on forever are minimal.

The same rule of calling the server's points first is used during the tiebreaker in tournament play. If an umpire is calling (refereeing) the match, he will usually add the name of the player serving next when calling the tiebreaker score. For example, he will say "Mr. X, 3 points to 4" (Mr. X will serve the next point).

During the tiebreaker the players change sides after each six points. Therefore, you change after 6 points, 12 points, 18 points and so on. After the tiebreaker is finished, a change of sides is mandatory.

In the first game of the following set, the next player at serve is the player who received the first point of the tiebreaker.

Posting the score of a set that went to a tiebreaker is done at 7–6 with the points scored in the tiebreaker in parenthesis, for example, 7–6 (10–8).

A final score for a match may look like this:

Mr. X   7–6 (9–7), 6–7 (10–12), 6–3.

The winner's games in each set are recorded first. Mr. X won the first set in a tiebreaker, lost the second set in another tiebreaker, then won the third set 6 games to 3.

13

Notes on Footwork and Timing

Playing the Rally Game gives you a good chance to streamline your footwork and timing.

Footwork in tennis is a very natural and simple thing. You turn your body toward wherever you have to run or walk, and you move your feet as if you were walking down the street or running to catch a bus.

If your opponent hits a short ball and you are facing it, you don't need to turn your feet. Just go straight to the ball and hit it. If the ball is hit to your side, turn that way, get to the ball, and strike it. If you need to cover the court you just left open, turn and go that way.

Slow ball? Go as slowly as you please. Fast ball? Go as quickly as needed.

If you want to get to the ball quickly, lean in that direction to get a faster start.

These are very simple techniques of movement that you probably learned before you were five years old.

Pivoting into the direction you want to go is crucial and the most natural thing you can do. I see very young children turning when they want to change the direction of their walk or their run, so I see no reason why adults can't also do it.

Leaning while pivoting is the fastest way of turning and starting to move, just like the basketball pros do. Top tennis pros do it very well, especially in stress situations. They take several sidesteps only when they have a lot of time or they want to stay in the vicinity of their last shot, not when they want to race all the way across the court.

Many professionals skip up and down on their toes between shots to keep their legs alert and ready for a fast start. You can do this sometime in your development, but beware: thinking of your feet can be very harmful to your game. As a beginner, don't complicate your learning. Just turn to the right or to the left, or wherever you have to go.

You want to strike the ball as comfortably as possible. Walking backward or to the side to get out of the way of a ball coming straight at you is okay. Backing up to let a high ball drop to where it is easier to handle is also fine. But if you have to go some distance, it is better to turn your feet in the direction you are going, while watching the ball over your shoulder. Then turn again to strike the ball as usual.

Lean, step, walk or run naturally, without paying attention to the position of your feet. Keep your attention on finding the ball.

Many people move their rackets in preparation for their shots long before they move their legs, wasting valuable time that should be used to get to the ball. Keep your arms close to your body while you run. When you are near the ball, you may move your arms away from your body to get momentum or reach, but well after your body has moved. Of course, you can pump your arms in your run if needed, but have the racket come back to both hands if possible before you get to the ball, in preparation for your shot.

There is a definite separation between the time you move your body, usually leaning and turning to get to the ball, and the time you swing. This sequence sometimes takes too short a time to really get the feet moving, because of the speed of play.

That is the reason why most top players split-step (a quick upward jump, with the feet landing about shoulder width apart), just as the opponent is about to strike the ball. That gives them momentum, like a coiled spring, to lean and start in any direction, anticipating the flight of the ball.

Anticipation

Anticipation is reading the racket-to-ball contact of your opponent. From his racket angle at impact point you know where the ball will go before it actually starts its flight toward your court.

If you carefully observe your opponent's racket at the moment it makes contact with the ball, this will become very apparent. Just leaning in the direction the ball is about to take will tilt your body and your weight that way and help you start to move.

Timing

Timing is the coordination between the time the ball is nearing your reach and the release of your stroke.

Correct timing by the professionals simply comes down to waiting for the right moment to strike the ball. That is why many pros use the left hand to hold on to the racket. It helps them wait. It makes them move their legs first, rather than overreacting with the arm alone.

The left hand also helps change the grip when necessary, simultaneous with the first shoulder turn.

As a last-minute effort to get to a difficult ball, a player will stretch the arm in a groundstroke or a volley. That occurs after the body has moved and the swing has started in a normal way.

On both the forehand and the two-handed backhand, if your arm or arms have to stretch to get to the ball, finish toward the opposite shoulder as you did on your easier shots. This will help your timing and ensure that the ball goes over the net and into the court.

Delicate touch shots, or blocking difficult returns, should be the only exceptions to this rule.

Preparing Early

Taking the racket back too early messes up both finding the ball and timing your hit. Most conventional teaching techniques discourage waiting and stress the earliest possible backswing. This makes it very difficult to find the ball well and to hit it with control.

Those techniques are outdated, as shown by the way the top pros play today. They may turn the shoulders, changing grip in the process, but the hands stay near the body, waiting for the right moment to swing.

In your groundstrokes, wait until after the bounce of the ball before you make a final judgment as to how you are going to swing.

Waiting longer actually seems to increase the time you have to make a perfect shot. Your mind may not grasp all the details, but at a deeper level you'll feel the difference.

Learn this from the beginning. Have your partner hit slow, looping balls. Keep both hands on your racket as long as possible. As you get faster balls you may tend to get anxious and overreact. Keep making yourself wait until well after the bounce. Move your feet and turn your shoulders in the process, but keep your hands near your body.

Wait for the bounce, then swing as usual, finishing your swing all the way.

In the one-handed backhand, the racket moves to a position parallel to the front of the body together with the shoulder turn. The racket head goes back, but beware of taking the arm back too soon.

In the forehand and two-handed backhand, the butt of the racket is kept close to the waist while turning and waiting for the bounce of the ball.

Wait and finish. No matter how horrified you may be that you might be late, keep yourself from overreacting.

Your legs may be racing all over the court, but wait until you are near the ball to move your arms to swing.

Most human beings tend to overreact. The top professionals wait—sometimes milliseconds—but they wait. That is why some pros seem almost inhuman—they are so cool, with such great timing.

Pros are as human as anyone. They have learned to wait, no matter how fast the ball is coming, no matter how anxious they may be. They have gotten so used to waiting that it seems totally natural to them.

The body reacts while the ball is still far away, the arm reacts when the ball is near. Sometimes it seems too late, but if you keep your mind on finding the ball and on the finish of the stroke, instinct takes over and you get the ball where you want it.

The Striking Zone

Most conventional techniques also stress hitting the ball well in front. There is quite a risk involved in that.

To explain further, the point where you meet the ball doesn't necessarily have to be exact or the same every time. There is an entire zone in which you can stroke the ball perfectly, provided that you first *find* it well. Attempt to almost touch it before exerting your force on the swing, making sure that you have angled the racket correctly for that particular shot.

The following diagram shows that the direction of your shot can remain the same in any of the contact points within the correct striking zone. The height of your shot can also remain constant, provided you didn't change the racket angle in this zone.

This correct striking zone can be, in your groundstrokes, as long as two feet. The front position (1) is in the area where it is easier to hit the ball flat, while (2) and (3) are better for topspin shots. It is easier at (2) and (3) to "muscle" the ball, keeping it on your strings longer, and rotating it more.

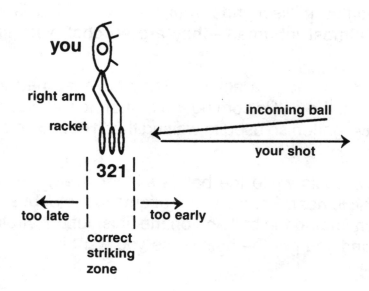

In coaching professionals and top junior players I make sure that the athlete hits many balls around (3) during practice. The tendency in tight spots in tournament play is to rush slightly. The player used to (3) will tend to hit at (2). The player used to hitting at (2) will tend to hit at (1), getting less topspin than he intended, possibly hitting out by a foot or two.

The player used to (1) will hit a few shots too early and the ball will sail out. The difference here may be just a few inches within the striking zone. In terms of time it could be a difference of just a few hundredths of a second. But in terms of feel, the difference is more pronounced. The impact is definitely longer when you let the ball come farther back and you "muscle" it with topspin.

You may hit a few balls too late through your learning period. You'll definitely notice those. But if you are constantly early you may not know what is going wrong. Diagnosing early shots is more difficult because of the compensations you may create to make up for it.

That is another good reason to wait for the ball as long as possible. The fewer the number of compensations, the smoother and simpler your swing will be, and you'll get more "feel."

The accuracy of a pro is so high when hitting within this latter part of the striking zone [between (2) and (3)], that the player gets very confident and goes for better and better shots, whether they are harder, at more of an angle, or closer to the lines.

Throughout this whole striking zone your racket angle should change as little as possible, so that your shot goes where you want even if you misjudge the contact point.

14

The Volley and Smash

The volley game is a major part of developing your game to championship standards.

No game is complete unless you know how to play any shot in any part of the court. Otherwise, an accomplished player could easily exploit any weaknesses in your game.

Most tournament players scout their opponents for obvious faults or unskilled areas in their game. One particular spot is vulnerability to short balls.

With the type of strokes you are learning here, it isn't difficult to attack short balls, make forceful approaches, and set yourself up to end the point at net with easy put-aways.*

There are two stages to learning the volley. The first is to become familiar with shots close to the net and above it.

After mastering those, you'll move away from the net, learning more difficult volleys, sometimes hitting the ball from below the level of the net.

This could be called the second level. Here you will learn the shots that will enable you to play an attack game, in which you could serve and volley or go to the net most of the time.

This requires a different type of proficiency on the volley, a different type of game. It is also a different dominion in terms of the space of the court, both your own and your opponent's, and it prac-

*Put-away: A shot hit from above net level that you can "put away" as a winner.

165

tically requires another state of mind. You want to rush your opponent, in order to cut his response time.

It is very different from your Rally Game, but it may be useful on faster courts or in cases where your steadiness from the baseline doesn't make a dent.

Because of all these reasons, I will introduce you to the volley slowly, building it one step at a time.

Consider it a major undertaking. Make sure you are proficient in each step before you tackle the next.

I also recommend that you master your put-aways by attacking short balls and following them to the net in your practice and matches. Get familiar with this type of volleying before you go to the sophistication of a more advanced serve-and-volley or an all-out attack game.

Then go to the section on advanced volley drills and practice those to your total satisfaction. In those drills you'll move gradually away from the net until you learn to volley from anywhere on the court.

Basic Concepts

All volleys, including low ones, are hit down and forward.

The most modern volleying, which is also the most effective, stops the hand and racket at contact with the ball, except for easy put-aways, where it follows through more.

This is a dramatic change from your groundstrokes. That is the reason you have to first become very proficient in your backcourt game, where it is important to follow through all the way.

You'll hit many balls from above the net level, where it seems logical to hit down. But when the ball drops below the top of the net you can also achieve great results by going down and forward with your racket, with the racket face sharply open.

Then stop the hand firmly at contact, like a cutting action with an ax.

The ball will clear the net and go forward at a good pace, making this shot very effective. The backspin will make the ball slide and stay low on your opponent's court.

High Volley   *Low Volley*

Advanced Players

You may be learning tennis through this book, or perhaps you have played for many years, but are not skilled at volleying. Regardless of your level of advancement, you can learn to be a good volleyer following the same path through the drills.

While someone starting to learn to volley may do a drill thirty or forty times before having it totally under control, an advanced player may accomplish the same for one drill in eight or ten repetitions. Perhaps the next drill would take much longer to accomplish, and so on.

Each drill develops a certain aspect of a shot, anything from co-ordination, control, racket angle, placement, etc. Do each drill until you feel you've got it. Keep the sequence as laid out in this chapter to get the best results (see **CAUTION** note on page 13).

On the other hand, if you have a good forehand volley and a poor backhand one, you can skip the first section and go directly to the backhand volley drills. Or if you have excellent high volleys and weaker lower ones, go to the low volley drills.

Professionals

For the very advanced player or pro, just reading this material may point to a concept previously not clearly defined or, perhaps, defined incorrectly. By analyzing this new data against your experience, you can envision the changes that need to be made.

Translate this into practice and observe the results. You can now decide whether to incorporate this new data into your game or keep the same old form.

Many times what seems tailor-made for one player may not fit another as well. Practice will tell you what is valuable for you and what is not.

The Forehand Volley

DRILL #1: Stand about two feet from the net, in the center. Have your friend stand at the other side of the net, about five feet away from it, and slightly to your left. He'll toss a ball to your right side, about face high.

Barehanded, block the ball down firmly with your right hand so that it clears the net and goes down in your opponent's court, as shown in the picture below.

Your hand should stop at the contact with the ball. Repeat several times. Block some balls in different directions just slightly changing the angle of your hand. Keep doing it until you are successful on every try.

DRILL #2: Grab your racket as shown in the picture on the next page, with your right hand behind the strings and the left hand midway on the throat. Block the ball the same way as in the prior drill.

Your hand needs to stay against the strings to get the feel that you are blocking the ball with your hand.

Try some balls in one direction, then in another, changing the angle of your right hand.

DRILL #3: After successfully performing the previous drill, move your right hand to the throat of the racket, with the tip of the fingers of your left hand on the throat, above the right hand, as shown in Picture 1 on the next page.

Block the ball down as shown in Picture 2, sending the ball over the net and down into the other court.

While waiting at the net or anticipating a volley, the racket head is held above hand level instead of at hand level or below, as in the groundstrokes.

Note that the left hand helps prepare the shot and lift the racket if necessary. It will let go of the racket prior to the hit, but will stay in the vicinity of the racket and will come back to it after each hit.

When the ball is coming toward your side and you need to move your body, it is best to lean first in that direction, then let go of the racket with the left hand just prior to the hit.

Let the ball come near your racket before you hit. Most errors are due to rushing, instead of waiting for the ball to come close and then blocking it firmly with the center of the racket strings. You'll actually hit in front, but striking too early will affect your consistency and control.

It is best to keep the racket face slightly open and to hit down on the ball, while still going forward, than to hit the ball plainly forward and flat. The slight backspin that you get by hitting down will add to your control.

As you progress, move your hand gradually toward the grip of the racket, volleying ten or twenty balls in each grip position. Don't rush these changes because it is easier to learn with the racket gripped short than with your hand all the way down to the grip.

DRILL #4: After mastering the last drill, with good control of the placement of your shots, move to a position about six to eight feet from the net and volley from there. Your friend needs to stay clear to one side so as not to get hit by your returns.

First, have your friend feed some higher balls, shoulder level or above.

When the ball comes high, it is a good idea to point to the incoming ball with the racket butt. This will automatically open the racket face, allowing you to hit down without hitting the ball into the net.

Lead the shot with your hand, rather than with the head of the racket.

(I have used this laid back position of the racket to correct many advanced players who had trouble with the forehand volley.)

Next, have your friend feed some lower balls. Open your racket face while you go down to find the ball. Lead the shot with the bottom edge of your racket, as shown in the picture below.

This is done while going forward and stopping at contact with a firm hit, as if you were stopping an ax at the contact with a tree.

The ball should come up and clear the net with some pace, but not too much backward rotation. Otherwise, it will be a slow shot.

Try some different racket positions to get a clue as to what the opening of your racket should be for each shot. There isn't a set racket angle. It all depends on how the ball is coming to you.

After you have the height and depth of your shots under control, have your friend stand in front of you. Practice hitting some balls to his right and some to his left. You'll need only to vary the angle of your racket, without changing your grip, to accomplish this. Again, practice will tell you the relationship between your racket angle and your placement.

The Backhand Volley

The most efficient volleyers volley all shots with their dominant hand. There is much more reach hitting the backhand volley with one hand, than by keeping both hands on the racket throughout.

Therefore, I will teach you the one-handed backhand volley first. Later in this chapter I will describe the two-handed backhand volley.

DRILL #1: Stand about two feet from the net and hold the racket from the throat with your left hand. Put the racket in front of you, a little to your left, about shoulder height, as shown in Picture 1 on the next page. Place the back of your right hand **behind** the strings.

Your friend tosses a ball toward your racket. Block it down into your opponent's court, keeping your hand against the strings (Picture 2). Repeat several times. This will give you the idea that hitting the backhand volley is like blocking it with the back of your hand.

DRILL #2: Grab the racket by the grip with your right hand, as shown in Picture 3, with your thumb against the back side. Have your left hand on the throat of the racket, holding it back. Now block the ball as shown in Picture 4, letting go of the racket from your left hand, as with a slingshot. Always hit down.

After each hit have the racket come back up and onto your left hand.

Note that a shoulder turn helps you hit more comfortably, especially when the ball goes farther away to your left.

Pointing the butt of the racket to the incoming ball (as shown in Picture 3) helps to find the ball and to hit it firmly. This pointing will also help you later to rotate the racket from a forehand volley to a backhand volley.

The racket movement for the hit comes from extending the arm, rather than breaking the wrist (see the following pictures).

Right   *Wrong*

DRILL #3: With your friend in front of you, but safely farther back, hit some balls to his right, then some to his left. Do this gently but firmly, varying the racket angle but not your grip. Repeat until you have complete control of your shot direction and you meet every ball in the center of your racket strings.

DRILL #4: Continue practicing, but slide your hand gradually toward the grip of the racket, until you get to a normal grip position (Picture 1, next page).

At this point it is better to move your thumb down and around the grip (Picture 2, next page), because the thumb against the back, although good for early developing stages, will make it difficult to open the racket face for very low volleys.

Practice volleying with this new grip, but make sure that you still can volley firmly on high balls, too. If you have trouble, keep your thumb against the back side until you strengthen your hand and your arm.

1   2

DRILL #5: Move away from the net another six to eight feet and volley from there until you have control. Then, have your friend feed you some higher balls. Point the butt of the racket to the incoming ball (Picture 1, below), then block it firmly (Picture 2, below).

1   2

Lead the shot with the butt of your racket, rather than with the racket head and breaking the wrist. As you hit, the right arm should extend toward the net. The left arm extends toward the backcourt to help you keep your balance, as shown in Picture 2.

Next, have your friend feed low balls. Open the racket face sharply and lead the shot with the bottom edge of your racket, like a cutting action, as shown in the next picture.

Hit down and forward. Stop firmly at contact with the ball, to send it over the net at a good pace.

You need to work out the correct angle of your racket to give good pace and some depth to your shot. If you cut it too much it will be a slow shot.

The angle of your racket should vary, depending on the speed and height of the ball coming to you. In the beginning, get the racket face almost parallel to the ground for very low balls. Then, start to adjust according to the results you get. This racket angling is learned from experience and instinct, rather than being set the same all the time.

Combining Forehand and Backhand Volleys

When you are waiting at the net for your opponent to hit the ball, you hold the racket in front of you. Whether you'll go to your right or to your left depends on the direction of your opponent's next shot.

In a previous chapter I described how to anticipate the direction of your opponent's next shot by carefully observing his racket angle the moment he makes contact with the ball. As soon as you see whether the ball is about to go to your right or to your left, lean in that direction.

Your upper body usually turns in that direction, too. Keep both hands on the racket during this turn to adjust the grip and line up your shot.

DRILL #1: Starting with slow balls, your friend alternates the toss to your right side and to your left.

Don't rush. Wait for the ball. Lean and turn slowly and deliberately, taking as much time as you can, instead of getting ready too fast. This way you'll move naturally. You'll work out what is necessary and what is not, what to focus on and what to ignore.

Going slowly will throw overboard those unnecessary details that will trap you at higher speeds. The slower you go at these slow ball speeds, while simplifying your moves, the faster and better you'll react to the high ball speeds.

Grip changes at the net for pros are minimal. They occur mostly at the bottom of the palm of the hand, while reacting to the right or to the left. I taught you more of a grip change to get you started. Later on, as you find the ball better and better, you'll achieve more firmness and certainty in your contact with the ball. By then you'll need less grip change in your volleys.

This latter stage is usually called the continental grip for your volleys, halfway between your regular forehand and one-handed backhand grips.

Some minor natural adjustments will occur—even with a continental grip—for both your forehand and backhand volleys to be truly efficient. Going from the right to the left, and vice versa, the racket angle will change slightly in your hand.

Again, it is the left hand's hold of the racket that induces these changes. It will pull the racket back with your left turn, then release it for the backhand volley, as shown in the next two pictures.

If you go for a forehand volley, push your racket toward your right with the left hand, together with an upper body turn to the right, as shown in the next two pictures, and you'll be ready for a firm block.

If you followed the drills and instructions detailed early in this chapter, this should now be built in at your instinct level.

The best volleyers volley firmly but not too hard. Hitting hard interferes with finding and feeling the ball.

You don't need to grip the racket tightly in between shots. Have the racket rest on the fingertips of your left hand, holding the racket head up. The right hand "feels" the grip, firm but not tight, and your body is ready to jump to find the ball. You start your move, releasing the left hand as late as you can. Then you hit, tightening up the racket at contact with the ball, stopping it firmly as you would stop a hammer hitting a nail. Then come back to the ready position, covering the court as best you can.

The Two-Handed Backhand Volley

If you truly feel that you like to hit the backhand volley with two hands, leave both hands on the racket, without any grip change.

Your hands will either be touching each other or fairly close together.

The racket face is held up while you wait for the ball. Then go for the ball and hit it forward and down, with a slight cut. Stop at contact, with the left hand doing most of the work.

This two-handed volley is similar to a forehand volley with your left hand, except that the right hand is kept on the racket. You can follow the same learning sequence you did for your forehand volley, but using your left hand instead. Grip your racket with the left hand higher on the grip to leave room to put your right hand at the end of the grip, rather than on the throat. In the beginning, alternate hitting one volley with the left hand, then one volley with both hands. After a while, keep the right hand on, but without letting it interfere with the work of the left hand.

In the two-handed backhand volley it is the left hand that changes the angle of the racket. The right hand accompanies it.

It is an easy stroke to develop, especially if you already have a two-handed backhand stroke. The only disadvantage is a big reduction in reach. The one-handed backhand volley allows an unequaled stretch for difficult shots, while this two-handed backhand volley does not. On the other hand, you may like the feel of the two-handed shot and its simplicity, since it doesn't require a grip change at all.

Hit down on low two-handed volleys, leading the shot with the bottom edge of the racket and with a sharply opened racket face. Stop firmly at contact, and the ball will clear the net safely and carry some good pace into the other side.

The Smash

When your opponent is trying to lob the ball over your head, you "smash" it directly overhead.

This smash requires only a short preparation, and it is similar to the serve described in the beginning of the service chapter.

DRILL #1: Stand close to the net. Have your friend toss balls to you a little higher than your head. Hit them down in your opponent's court with your right hand, as shown in the picture on the next page.

DRILL #2: Have your friend stand safely to one side. Grab your racket as shown in the next picture, with the right hand behind the strings. Your friend again tosses the ball above your head and you hit them down in your opponent's court, as if you were hitting them with your right hand.

Do this gently, with control. Find the ball well and hit away from your friend to avoid hitting him.

Smashes are hit down, rather than up like serves. They are also much more flat.

DRILL #3: Grab your racket by the throat. When going up for the ball, also lift the racket with your left hand, as shown in Picture 1. Find the ball well (Picture 2) and hit it down into your opponent's court (Pictures 3 & 4).

1   2   3   4

Unlike a fully developed serve with the long loop before going for the hit, the racket goes straight up as in the high forehand volley. Then maneuver yourself under the ball, finding it well, and hit it downward firmly, but with control.

DRILL #4: Have your friend feed higher balls. The left hand will become instrumental in placing yourself under the ball and finding it well.

Get yourself under the ball as well as possible, lifting the racket with both hands toward your right shoulder (Picture 1, page 183). Now point to the ball with your left hand (Picture 2), as if you were going to catch it, fine tuning your position below the ball at this time. Your racket has dropped behind your back, as in the serve. Find the ball well, then release your power into the shot (Picture 3), finishing toward your left hip (Picture 4).

This last detail is important to prevent you from hitting your legs with the racket.

DRILL #5: After becoming proficient in the former drill, move your hand gradually toward the racket grip. Hit several balls from each hand position, mastering the new racket length before going on to the next.

Follow through firmly but not hard, always ending with the throat of the racket in your left hand.

The most important thing in the smash is to find the ball well. The easiest place to do that is above your head, perhaps slightly in front and to the right. On most balls you will need to adjust to wherever the ball is going, whether it's to your right, to your left, or behind you.

The best smashers lift the racket with both hands, coordinated with the upward flight of the ball. Then, with the ball descending, they point to it with the left hand, as if going to catch it. Then they hit it. If the lob is clearly going back beyond their reach, instead of backpedaling, they turn their feet to run back normally, while still raising the racket slowly and looking at the ball over their left arm. When the ball is within their reach, they jump with a scissors-type leg action, which allows a timely power release and avoids hard lower back twisting or a harmful fall.

Smashes don't need much force to be fast. They require coordination and timing, with the force coming in when almost touching the ball. Smashes usually come out harder than intended, especially in the early learning stages.

For your friend's safety, smash gently and with control.

Learning the Smash by Yourself

If you don't have a friend who can hit high balls to you, you can toss them high yourself and do the drills described before. Just toss them high enough so that they clear your head after the bounce. Find the ball well as it starts to come down for the second time, and hit into your opponent's court.

Advanced players sometimes practice this way. They hit the ball up with the racket, let it bounce, go up again, then smash it down into the other court.

Again, should you do this, learn control rather than force. The force is within you—the control has to be learned.

Advanced Volleying

There are four major types of championship styles. One is the purely defensive player, who stays back as much as possible, and often just goes to the net to shake hands at the end of the match.

The next type of player is mostly a baseliner, but as soon as he gets a short ball, he hits a very forceful approach shot, almost a winner in itself, and gets to the net for a volley put-away.

The third type is the player who is skillful from the back, but who is always looking to maneuver to the net. He'll take more chances of going forward, and is usually good at placing the first volley where the opponent has difficulty making a good passing shot.

The last category is that of the serve-and-volley player who does it as a way of life, regardless of the surface. He probably isn't very skilled at matching groundstrokes from the backcourt, and usually thinks of it as a waste of time. Rather than work his way into the point, this player risks everything, from groundstrokes to storming the net on any kind of ball.

This can be very effective on given days, when things go right and the opponent collapses under the sheer pressure of the attack. But if this player is matched against a skilled all-court player, he'll have a struggle on his hands. The backcourt player will dampen the other player's attack with low angles and skilled lobs mixed with some forceful passing shots. Although backcourt players do more running, they do so with more time to get to the ball, while the attacking player depends mostly on jumping and lunging ability.

On clay courts, where matches between players of comparable skill usually go on for hours, an attacking player will have difficulty sustaining the effort for an entire match.

At championship level, serve-and-volley players get to most of their opponent's service returns near their own service line. The shot from here, should they be able to reach it before the bounce, is called the first volley. In most cases, the ball is by then below the level of the net. This first volley needs placement, pace, and depth. After hitting the first volley the player continues to advance toward the net, and is now prepared to cut off the next return, usually a forceful passing shot or a lob.

The attacking player is now in a more commanding position, but here the options for the opponent vary according to the type of surface of the court. On a slippery surface like grass, good players go for a forceful passing shot most of the time, or for a very defensive lob. The attacking player just needs to angle the next volley to the open court, and most likely it will be out of the other player's reach. On a lob, he needs to reach the ball and hit it to the open court.

But on slower surfaces, like clay courts and most modern championship hard courts, the likelihood of the defensive player hitting a good lob is much greater. The attacking player cannot risk getting very close to the net. He therefore opens himself to some angled passing shots.

Here is where an accomplished serve-and-volley player has something that the accomplished backcourt player does not: a sense of net coverage, of which angles to open and which ones to close. Serve-and-volley players know how to lure the opponent into hitting a particular shot. They can close the net fast, while still preparing to smash even a decent lob. A little while into the match, they've learned to anticipate the passing shot by reading the racket angle of the opponent at contact time. It is a skill that you develop by committing to a volley game. Your tactical approach changes, adjusting to different conditions that you create for yourself.

One major aspect of the successful attacking game is the pressure put on the opponent to make very good shots, which leads to many errors, especially in important points. The faster the court, the more pressure the player under attack feels.

The Low Volley at Championship Level

For a low volley, you obviously have to lower the racket from the normal height where you were holding it to the point where you'll meet the ball. You can use this downward (and at the same time forward) movement to get momentum to hit the ball. You get it to go over the net by opening the racket face, while you stop at contact with a firm grip. This will give the ball good speed, while it will still be accurate and clear the net. The ball will also have some backspin that will keep it low after it bounces in your opponent's court.

You can use this low volley with spectacular results from anywhere in the court, including being caught behind the service line or somewhere in the backcourt. The ball may be at your feet, without a bounce, and you can still make a good shot.

To develop this volley I have some interesting drills, for which you'll need someone good across the net to feed you the ball pretty low, reaching you at a height around knee level or below. You will also need a bucket with a minimum of twenty or thirty balls.

I have included these drills in this chapter, although they belong to an advanced level of play, because I know players of many different skill levels will read this book. At some point you may desire to learn this and it is available here for you to learn whenever you want. Even some of the most advanced players need to polish their strokes, and these drills will help them.

The Drills

In the diagram on the next page, FR, FC, and FL indicate each position where your friend will stand to feed the ball to you. **FR** is your **F**riend to your **R**ight, **FC** is your **F**riend in the **C**enter, and **FL** your **F**riend to your **L**eft. 1, 2, 3, 4, 5, and 6 are the positions where you will be, according to each particular drill.

R, L, and C are your target areas. **R** and **L** are the deep **R**ight and **L**eft corner areas of the court, and **C** is the deep **C**enter area of the court.

Mark these three areas with ropes, cones, or empty cans. On a clay court you can mark them with your foot.

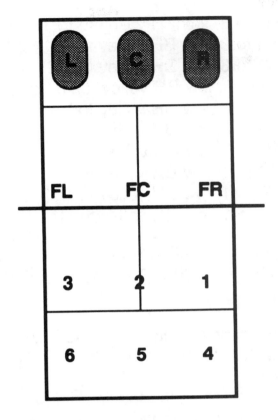

In the following drills, for example, FR to 2, Low FH volley to L means your friend stands at FR, you are at 2, he hits a ball to you toward your forehand side at knee level or below, you hit a forehand volley to the left corner area. On another drill, FL to 3, low BH volley to R means your friend is at FL, you are at 3, and you hit a low backhand volley to the right corner area.

Depending on your advancement, do each drill until you hit five, ten, or twenty balls in the area of your intended aim.

DRILL #1: FL to 1, low FH volley to C.
DRILL #2: FC to 1, low FH volley to R.
DRILL #3: FR to 1, low FH volley to L.
DRILL #4: FL to 2, low FH volley to R.
DRILL #5: FL to 2, low FH volley to C.
DRILL #6: FR to 2, low FH volley to L.
DRILL #7: FL to 3, low FH volley to R.
DRILL #8: FR to 3, low FH volley to C.

DRILL #9: FC to 3, low FH volley to L.
DRILL #10: FR to 3, low BH volley to C.
DRILL #11: FC to 3, low BH volley to L.
DRILL #12: FL to 3, low BH volley to R.
DRILL #13: FR to 2, low BH volley to L.
DRILL #14: FR to 2, low BH volley to C.
DRILL #15: FL to 2, low BH volley to R.
DRILL #16: FR to 1, low BH volley to L.
DRILL #17: FR to 1, low BH volley to C.
DRILL #18: FC to 1, low BH volley to R.

After completing these drills, repeat drills 1 through 9 hitting one forehand volley, one backhand volley, another forehand volley, and so on for each drill.

After you are successful volleying these low balls from the 1, 2, and 3 positions, switch to the backcourt.

Volleying from the 4, 5, and 6 positions, repeat drills 1 through 9 with the one forehand volley, one backhand volley routine, aiming to R, L, and C.

As soon as you feel good control hitting your low volley from anywhere in the court, your next step is to learn to hit while moving forward.

Stand on the baseline, behind 5. Hit your first volley at 5, your next one at 2, then get to the net and put the next volley away. For your next try go back to the baseline, behind 5 or 6, hit your first low backhand volley at 6, then a low volley at 2, then a put-away in front of 1 or 3. Mix positions in any way you like, forehand and backhand volleys alike, also mixing your aims to R, L, and C.

When you get good at moving around the court while volleying, add a smash to end each sequence. Some of the most advanced players continue the sequence through several hits. The player feeding the ball draws them back by hitting a deep lob. The next shot is a low one, drawing the player forward again.

I advise you not to try to learn all this in one day, unless you are a highly trained tournament player. Practice while you feel good and strong. When you get tired, save the rest of the drills for another day. Most professionals are so superbly conditioned that this type of tennis seems easy to them, but it causes a lot of physical stress to newer players.

McEnroe

John McEnroe has probably been the best volley player of all time. Although he has slowed down with age, he is still outstanding on low volleys, high volleys, delicate stop volleys, put-aways, smashes, anticipating and cutting off difficult passing shots—anything that he can catch on the fly.

McEnroe's body moves are very efficient, both in getting to the ball and stroking it. On the volley, he leads and leans with the upper body to wherever he has to go, getting a fast start. When he gets to the ball, he may jump or take a small hop, while his arm hits down and forward. At contact, he immediately stops the movement of his hand.

The combination of these last two features is what makes McEnroe so outstanding. What he achieves is to keep the center of the racket strings on the line of flight of the ball for a prolonged period of time, still discharging plenty of power into the hit. He avoids costly off-center mis-hits that dramatically affect the accuracy and speed of the shot and he doesn't depend on perfect timing at all.

Many of the world's best players mis-hit some volleys under pressure or when they want to put a lot of power into the shot. They either don't always time the volley properly, or their body interferes with the shot.

Most of these errors come from missing the intersection of the line of travel of the racket center with the ball's line of flight. The ball stays up while your racket goes down on your hit. Hit a little off-center, and your volley doesn't go exactly where you want.

McEnroe avoids that by lifting his body, which keeps the racket head on the line of the ball while he strokes. It is interesting to note that, even on his off days, when things seem to go wrong, his volley stays at a high level, and usually saves him from painful defeats.

Stopping the hand at contact with the ball is the other safety feature of McEnroe's technique. The stopping action will last a few tenths of a second, during which time the ball will hit the strings. On very fast passing shots, it is practically impossible to time the beginning of the stopping action at the point of impact with the ball.

At 65 mph, for example, the ball travels close to 100 feet per second. If your opponent is near his baseline and you are near the net, your distance is forty to forty-five feet. The ball will take approximately $5/10$ of a second to get to your racket. Your stopping action should commence just prior to contact with the ball, and will last throughout. The ball will be in your racket and out while you are still stopping it.

Therefore, just like McEnroe, you won't have any difficulty timing your hit. Although it feels different, that fast ball will hit your strings, rather than you hitting the ball. The resulting shot placement will depend on your racket face angle, which of course you control with the position of your hand.

This type of advanced volleying is easy to learn. First look for the ball, leaning toward it with your upper body or your head. If the ball is hard and stays up, pull your head upward together with your downward hit, or move your face away from the ball, stopping your hand firmly inches *before* the hit. If you are moving forward, try a little jump or a hop.

Otherwise, if the ball is a "sinker" (dropping quickly), lower your trunk, but hop forward as you hit it. On these, as well as on the high volley or a slow passing shot, you can discharge more power. Stop your action *during* the hit. At least get the sensation that you are stopping your arm. By then the ball is gone from your racket but your accuracy will improve. On an easy set-up, stop your arm *right after* the hit.

The results of this technique are astounding. The hits are firm and accurate. With some practice, you'll hit the ball consistently in the center of your racket strings, allowing you to develop great racket control and touch.

Do not stroke too early. While volleying, you should keep your playing hand in front and you should hit in front. But releasing your power too soon or stopping too early will cause mistakes.

Perfect timing is waiting for the right moment to hit. Sometimes it seems there isn't enough time. You feel rushed. But with practice you'll be able to "feel" the difference between too early and too late. You'll time your stopping action according to the speed of the incoming ball.

15

Special Shots

The Backhand Slice

The backhand slice, whether one-handed or two-handed, is a backhand swing hit from high to low with the racket face sharply opened. It is similar to the backhand volley, except that you accelerate from the ball forward, continuing well past the ball, while in the volley you stop as you hit.

By hitting down and forward, and leading the stroke with the bottom edge of the racket, you brush underneath the ball and make it spin backward, as shown in the diagram.

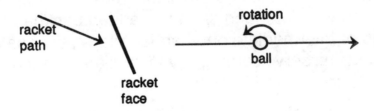

This is the opposite of topspin, and is called underspin or slice.

This spin creates more air friction at the bottom of the ball than on the top, keeping it in the air longer. The ball tends to fly more on a straight line than on a pronounced downward curve, as in topspin shots.

To compensate, slice groundstokes have to be hit lower than top-spin shots, with a smaller clearance over the net or they will go out of bounds.

Professionals usually return fast serves with this slice backhand because it can be shortened, blocking the return, and still get ball speed and accuracy. You can also keep the ball low and get some depth, which makes this slice return effective whether your opponent serves and comes straight to the net or stays back.

If the serve comes to your forehand it is a different story, because you can hit a forehand hard with topspin with no preparation. A very hard return will give your opponent trouble even if it doesn't go very deep.

This is also true for the two-handed backhand, which doesn't need any preparation prior to the hit. You jump at that fast serve and follow through hard, up and over the ball.

On the one-handed backhand return you need more preparation, such as a shoulder turn and a backhand grip, to drive through the ball.

A top pro may wait for a first serve favoring his one-handed backhand side, and slam a hard flat or topspin backhand return, surprising his opponent on his way to the net. But it is a risky shot that requires tremendous skill and precision. You can't muscle the ball as well as with your forehand or a two-handed backhand. If you are a beginning or intermediate one-handed player, your safest choice for a booming first serve coming to your backhand is a blocked slice return.

While rallying, a slice backhand hit low and firm can give trouble to your opponent by skidding and staying low. It all depends on your opponent's adjustment to different strokes. Some players like to hit their groundstrokes with the ball low, others higher.

You may prefer one style of backhand over the other. If you feel that you can do better with just one type of stroke, I wouldn't disturb that feeling. Your confidence depends on what *you* feel about your game, not what others think about it.

On the other hand, adding this slice stroke to your repertoire will make you a more complete player, helping you vary your strokes when needed, mixing up slices with topspin strokes.

Personally, I consider this backhand easy and effective. Many of my students, taught flat one-handed backhands, have drifted naturally towards a slice stroke.

Learning this stroke is easy. To start, you only have to point the butt of the racket at the incoming ball to be ready. The racket face stays open, as shown in the picture below.

This will automatically change your grip to the backhand. The grip change doesn't need to be as pronounced as for the topspin backhand. Your fingers stay spread apart, as in the forehand grip.

The main change occurs at the bottom of the hand, which gets slightly mounted on the top bevel of the butt of the grip.

The best way to cause this grip change is to pull from the throat of the racket with the left hand while pointing the butt of the racket to the ball. This brings the racket to a position closer to perpendicular with your right forearm.

On a fast ball, this is all the backswing you need, pulling the racket with your left hand toward your left side. You'll be able to block the ball instinctively with a short stroke.

Your elbow needs to separate from your body. On the easier or slower ball, when you are preparing for a longer stroke, the arm is usually bent at the elbow, and the stroke is done by extending the arm past the contact with the ball.

In the beginning, it is a good idea to point both the butt of the racket and your elbow to the incoming ball, while still holding the racket with both hands. Then straighten your right arm at the elbow, putting separation between the arms. (See picture sequence below.)

The backhand slice

The left arm should stretch back to keep your balance and to prevent you from turning too early to your right, which could vary the shot direction from your intended aim.

The height of your shot will depend on how much your racket face is open. While learning, keep the racket face angle quite open and hit down on the ball. Make it very different from your topspin stroke, so you do not get them confused.

Two-Handed Slice

If you have a two-handed backhand and also want to slice the ball using both hands, simply open the racket face, find the ball well, and hit from high to low.

Practice will tell you all the refinements as to racket angle and spin. There are no complications or secrets. On your topspin, close the racket face and hit up. On your slice, open the racket face and hit down.

Some of the top pros have a two-handed topspin backhand but use a one-handed backhand slice. You can also do this by pulling from the throat of the racket with your left hand as you turn to your left, pushing away with your right hand, and pointing the butt of the racket to the incoming ball. This will automatically get the backhand slice grip in your right hand, and will also give more firmness to your stroke than if you keep the forehand grip.

Even if you are strictly a two-hander in your backhand, you should practice the one-handed slice. In some situations it is very difficult or even impossible to get to the ball with both hands on the racket. If you have practiced a one-handed backhand slice, you'll instinctively reach for the ball this way and possibly keep the ball in play, saving you from a certain point loss.

To develop this stroke, do the drills shown in Chapter Nine on the one-handed backhand. Nothing should be different, except your style. You are slicing under the ball now, while before you were hitting up.

High Backhands

Most one-handed players have trouble when the ball comes high to their backhand side. Two-handers can drive the ball back hard before it goes up high, or may back up to let it come down to a height where they can drive it.

One-handed players don't have much power when hitting a high ball to their backhand, and usually hit a weak return on that shot. But if you have a backhand slice, there is a simple technique that allows you to put power and depth into this shot.

First, with the racket still in both hands, point the butt of the racket to the incoming ball, as shown in Picture 1 below.

1   2   3

When the ball gets close to you, extend your arms, as shown in Picture 2, bringing the head of the racket to meet the ball.

Follow through strongly from the ball forward, until your arms are fully extended as in Picture 3.

The resulting shot is actually a slice backhand, and the ball carries speed that makes it go deep.

You may use your body to add power to this shot. It actually depends on your "feel" for the particular situation. This shot needs to be practiced to develop your "feel" for it, as well as to strengthen your shoulder and back muscles.

The Lob

The lob is a ball hit high to send it above the reach of a player near the net.

With the type of topspin strokes you learned earlier, you just need to lift the ball higher to get a good lob. Open the racket face, still hitting with topspin, and lift the ball fifteen to twenty feet over the net.

Although the ball may be slower than a hard groundstroke, you still need plenty of racket speed and a lot of topspin. This will make the ball bounce past your opponent's service line.

The topspin will help get the ball down sooner and faster and make it jump toward the back fence. It will then be difficult, if not impossible, for your opponent to get to the ball.

This shot was very unusual some twenty years ago, but today it is very common among the top pros.

Another way of achieving a lob—very useful when reaching the ball with great difficulty—is simply to open the racket face under the ball and hit it up. It will probably be a slow ball, but if you hit it 25 feet or more in the air and deep into your opponent's court, it will give you time to get back to a more comfortable position in your court. This shot is usually called a "defensive" lob.

The deeper you hit a defensive lob into your opponent's court, the more difficulty he'll have in handling it and smashing it back.

The Half Volley

The half volley is not really a volley, but a short groundstroke hit immediately after the bounce of the ball.

It is a delicate shot, but necessary when you are caught near the bounce of the ball and can't volley it on the fly.

If the ball is about to bounce close to you, get your racket behind the bounce and time your hit to start with the bounce, practically from the ball forward, with no backswing at all.

Finding the ball is done at the same time you accelerate your hand with a lift. Hit upward, letting the racket flow naturally and over the ball, slightly covering it with the racket face. This will keep the ball low and quick, preventing it from shooting up and giving your opponent an easy set up.

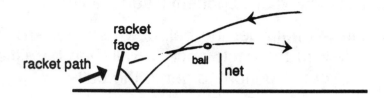

The most critical thing here is the timing and the racket angle. Feel that you are coming off the ground together with the ball and that you brush up on it, covering the ball as if you had your hand slightly over it.

You can either finish the stroke as usual or make a much shorter motion. Either one will work as long as you find the ball perfectly with a pick-up action, your body timed to come up at the same time.

For both the forehand and the two-handed backhand half volleys, hit the ball close to your side, rather than well in front. On the one-handed backhand, hit it more in front.

The Drop Shot

The drop shot is a short ball that you hit to your opponent to put it out of his reach, to force him to make an error, or to get him out of position so that you can hit a winner past him.

To keep your opponent unaware of your next shot, fake it, as if you were about to hit a groundstroke. Just when you are about to hit, change it to a drop shot.

The drop shot is a delicate move, more like caressing the ball than like striking it. In essence, there is no backswing to the drop shot, but a very sharp opening of the racket face, while advancing the racket across the bottom of the ball, gently touching its back and underside, as shown in this diagram.

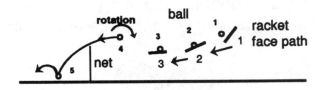

Follow through well past the ball. Make the ball underspin (backspin) and curve over the net, just enough to clear it. It will land softly on the other side, and the backspin will make it stop quickly, usually with a short bounce.

The drop shot feels the same for the forehand as well as the one-handed and two-handed backhands. Your grip on the racket has to be softened during the impact depending on your distance from the net. The closer to the net, the softer your shot needs to be.

The ability to hit soft shots is called a player's "touch," usually developed with much practice and experience. The better you find the ball, the more "touch" you'll develop.

The Stop Volley

The stop volley (or touch volley) is a volley hit softly, stopping the ball very short and close to the net in your opponent's court.

It is a great shot to hit when you have your opponent deep to one side and you are at the net. Delicately touch the ball in the other direction and he will never get to the ball.

You can disguise it as a regular volley and at the last possible moment open your racket face sharply, as in the drop shot, and soften your grip. The ball will not gain any momentum and will bounce softly off your racket, curving over the net, and "dying" in your opponent's court.

Feel that you stop your hand, right at the impact, while your racket head drops, face opened, touching the underside of the ball. It is like the drop shot action, except there is no followthrough.

16

Drills for Development

When a ball comes toward you, either to your forehand or backhand side, you have only three choices of direction in which to hit it back—down the line, crosscourt, or down the middle.

You must also choose to hit it short or long, high or low, or somewhere in between. There aren't a million choices, so you don't have to think much. Brilliance in tennis is usually the player's combination of instinct and experience.

The best professionals, whether intelligent or not, do not rely on thinking while playing but on instinct and feeling. They have drilled or executed their down-the-line or crosscourt shots so many times that it is simple for them to decide where to hit, and to send the ball there.

They instinctively know where to hit—especially if they wait to make that decision until they see how the ball is coming at them, or how it has bounced. The more they delay their final decision on exact direction and height, the better they find the ball, and then, when they have the ball within their grasp, they make their decision and hit it there.

It is almost unbelievable how long you can wait before committing yourself. For example, you can get to the point that you are preparing to hit a down-the-line passing shot, and then, when you are almost touching the ball, change your mind and hit it crosscourt. Your opponent certainly is misguided by your early actions and usually gets caught going the wrong way. This, of course, is at a very high level of play. But you need to be aware from the beginning that waiting is far more valuable than rushing.

Drills

Drills are the best way to develop the feel of one shot direction at a time so that you know where your shot is going.

It will also be easier to decide where to hit each shot, as drills let you know your margin for error. For example, you observe in a drill that your forehand down the line goes off a maximum of two feet to either side of your intended placement. In a match you'll know to aim at least two feet inside the court. The same would go for depth, taking into account that there is less control for the length of your shot than for direction.

In these drills you need another player with good control feeding you the balls. You should have a whole bucket of balls, and have them fed to you in a precise sequence, to simulate playing conditions and avoid unnecessary interruptions.

In most drills your friend will be standing to one side of the court. You have to aim your shots to the open space of the court, not back at your friend. This way you'll develop the idea of hitting to the open court instead of sending the ball back to where your opponent is standing and making his job easier.

Definitions

Down-the-line shot: A shot hit almost parallel to the sidelines. If both players are right-handed, you hit from your forehand to your opponent's backhand, or from your backhand to your opponent's forehand (lines 1 and 2).

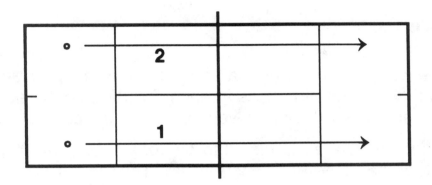

Crosscourt shot: A shot that you hit across the court. If both players are right-handed, you hit your forehand to your opponent's forehand, or your backhand to your opponent's backhand (lines 3 and 4).

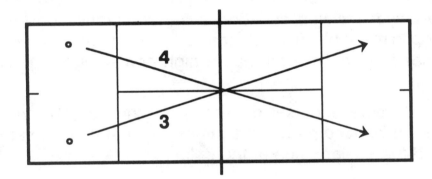

Down the middle shot: A ball you hit toward the middle of your opponent's court (lines 5, 6, and 7).

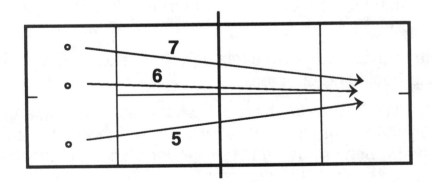

The Drills

Depending on your physical conditioning and your advancement, hit twenty to thirty balls in each drill. With some advanced players and professionals, I have used up to fifty balls per drill.

All these drills are not meant to be done in one day. If you get tired, stop and come back another day. The idea is to build your conditioning and stamina a little at a time while grooving-in your shots.

The same goes for the degree of difficulty that the feeder creates with a shorter or longer time lapse between shots, as well as with the placement and pace of delivery. The person feeding the balls is really "the coach" and is at the service of the student. He's helping the player develop confidence and assurance on his shots, not trying to make him miss. Accordingly, he should adjust his delivery to see that the student has a high percentage of successful shots.

Unpredictable increases of pace or difficulty are okay while drilling a very advanced player or a professional, but only after he has mastered the easier stage of the drill.

For the first five drills, use a can of balls or another marker in the middle of the court. Put the can behind the service line if you are a new player, inside the baseline if you are an intermediate player, or behind the baseline if you are very advanced. Always round the can from the back of the court and turn facing your opponent's court.

Some of these drills are explained more extensively in the forehand and backhand chapters.

DRILL #1: Topspin forehands down the line, running around the can after each shot. Turn left after your forehand shot, turn right after running behind the can. The feeder stands across the net to your left, as shown in the diagram.

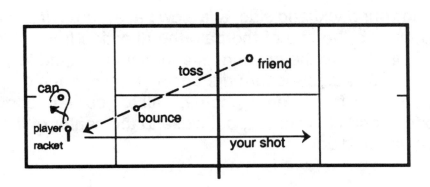

DRILL #2: Topspin forehands crosscourt, running around the can after each shot. The feeder stands across the net to your right.

DRILL #3: Topspin backhands down the line, running around the can after each shot. The feeder stands across the net to your right, as shown in the diagram.

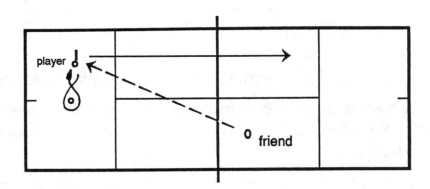

DRILL #4: Topspin backhands crosscourt, running around the can after each shot. The feeder stands across the net to your left.

DRILL #5: Backhand slice, alternating one shot down the line and one crosscourt, running around the can after each shot. The feeder stands across the net in the middle of the court, behind his service line.

DRILL #6: Forehand topspin inside out, avoiding your backhand and going back to the middle after each shot. Start from the middle of the court, without the can. Your friend tosses a ball about three to four feet to your backhand side, at a slow pace. Turn left toward that side, go beyond the line of the ball (the direction from which it is coming), turn toward the net and hit a topspin forehand to your opponent's backhand court. Turn right after your shot and go back to the middle. Your friend feeds another ball to your left, and so on. The feeder stands to your left, but close to the center of the court, as shown in the diagram.

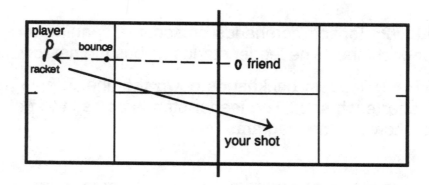

This is a stressful drill, especially if you don't turn properly.

The following drills are also done without the can of balls. The feeder will feed balls one to each side, back and forth, but not too quickly.

DRILL #7: Forehand down the line, backhand down the line. The feeder stands across the net, in the middle of the court, as shown in the diagram.

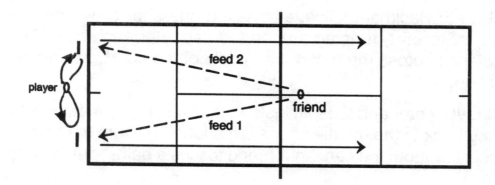

DRILL #8: Forehand crosscourt, backhand down the line. The feeder stands across the net to your right.

DRILL #9: Forehand down the line, backhand crosscourt. The feeder stands across the net to your left.

DRILL #10: Forehand crosscourt, backhand crosscourt. The feeder stands across the net, in the middle of the court, behind his service line.

DRILL #11: Volleys. Get near the net. Hit your forehand volley down the line and backhand volley crosscourt. The feeder stands in front of his baseline and to your left.

DRILL #12: Volleys. Forehand volley crosscourt, backhand volley down the line. The feeder stands in front of his baseline and to your right.

DRILL #13: Smash to the right side. You are near the net and the feeder stands to your left, close to his baseline. He hits lobs to you, and you smash to the open court.

DRILL #14: Smash to the left side. The feeder stands to your right, close to his baseline. He hits lobs to you, and you smash to the open court.

A good variation on the smash drill is to run up to the net after each smash, then run back to hit the next one, and so on.

Overall, keep the ball safe and over the net. On the groundstroke drills it is a good idea to hang a string two or three feet above the net. Except for the sliced backhand and passing shots, all other groundstrokes should clear this string. Even hard shots will go down in your opponent's court if you hit them with enough topspin.

Service Drills

For the next few drills divide each service court in half, as shown in the diagram on the next page. Place a can of balls in each half as shown, or any other marker. On a clay court you can mark a line with your foot. This will give you four areas to serve to, indicated in the diagram as 1, 2, 3, and 4.

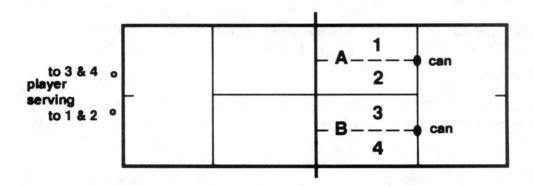

If you are playing a right-hander, when you serve to 1 or 3 you are serving to his forehand. When you serve to 2 or 4, to his backhand.

The first court you serve to in a match is to your left (A in the diagram). It is called the deuce court (see Chapter Twelve on scoring) because that's where your serve has to land when playing the deuce point. The service court to your right (B in the diagram) is called the ad (advantage) court.

DRILL #1: Serve twenty balls to the deuce court, to your opponent's backhand (area 2 in the diagram). Use your American Twist or your spin second serve.

DRILL #2: Serve twenty balls to the ad court, to your opponent's backhand (area 4 in the diagram), using your American Twist or your spin second serve.

DRILL #3: Serve twenty balls to the deuce court, to your opponent's forehand (area 1 in the diagram). Here, use more of a slice serve to pull the ball and the other player off the court.

DRILL #4: Serve twenty balls to the ad court, to your opponent's forehand (area 3 in the diagram). Use a slice serve to pull the ball away from your opponent.

I have instructed you to first serve to your opponent's backhand because that shot is usually weaker than his forehand. It is also your primary choice for your second serve. The placement, speed and kick of your second serve is probably more important than your cannonball first serve. At many important stages in your service games you may want to throw a safe kicker rather than risking a hard serve.

Hitting over a string two to three feet above the net is a valuable practice tool to keep your second serves safe and deep. You'll learn that serving up with spin makes the ball come down before the service line, while still kicking up high and fast.

One way to jam an opponent's return is to serve into his body. The exact placement varies with your opponent's skill. With some players you hit to the body, some to the right hip or shoulder, others to the left. Some are vulnerable to the high kicker, some to the slice.

You can try some different serves in the beginning of a match, then stick to the option that gives your opponent the most trouble. With some very skillful players none of these options to the body are very effective, and you have to resort to placing a high kicker on their backhand as your first serve in the closest scoring situations. Otherwise, should you risk your first serve and miss, your opponent may take command of the point with a very forceful return off your second serve.

Once you have practiced and mastered your second serve, practice your hard serves, mixing them up as you like, to the four areas shown in the diagram.

Advanced Drills

There are many advanced drills, some of which can be done with someone feeding balls from a bucket, others by simply hitting back and forth.

With someone feeding balls from a bucket, you can do a combination such as an approach shot (to approach the net), then a couple of volleys and a smash off the feeder's lob. On these drills, have the feeder stand to one side and hit toward the open court.

Another drill is to hit "behind" your opponent, sending the ball to the place your opponent just left. You can do this with the ground-stroke drills 1, 2, 3, 4, 8, 9, 11, and 12. Hit the ball to the small space between the feeder and the sideline closest to him, instead of to the open court. Your friend should stand a little more toward the center of the court than in the original drill, to leave you a slightly larger opening, depending on how advanced you are. It is best to disguise your shot by "pretending" you are about to hit the open court, then change your aim at the last possible moment and hit "behind." Disguising your shots will keep your opponent off balance, unable to read where you are really about to hit.

You can also do many drills hitting back and forth, but the effectiveness will depend on both players' levels of advancement. For example, one of the players can be at the net and to his right, covering just half of the singles court, while the other player is back. The volley player hits away from the backcourt player, who has to cover the whole court and hit all balls toward the player at the net.

In the next drill the player at the net moves to the left half of the singles court and volleys from there, while the backcourt player still covers his whole court, and hits back to the player at the net.

To become proficient at the net, have your friend stand in his backhand corner, just behind the baseline, while you cover the whole net and direct your volleys toward your friend. For the next drill, your friend should stand in his forehand corner and you direct your volleys there.

These last drills can be combined with lobs and smashes to get the net player away from the net and then back in for the next volley. Keep a good supply of balls in a bucket by the center of the court. The bucket and the singles sideline will be the boundary of the half court, determining the area where the player at the net has to hit all his shots.

One of the most strenuous drills, especially when done between two pros or very advanced players, is with both players back, one in a corner and the other covering the whole court. The player in the corner hits the ball from side to side, while the other player returns everything back to the same corner. It is a great conditioner for the legs and for the lungs, but should only be tried by young tournament players in great shape, and only for short periods of time. As with other stressful drills with one player stationary and the other covering the whole court, you can switch back and forth after each drill to give each other a rest.

The better the players, the more intense and more tiring these drills can be. You can devise other drills in which to practice your drop shot, your half volley, your serve and your service return.

A good way to practice your doubles game is to play points crosscourt, using only opposite halves of the court. You first serve from your right and your friend can only play to your right half of the court, all the way to the doubles line. Likewise, you have to continue the point hitting only to the half court to your opponent's right. The next point you serve from your left and you both play crosscourt to the opposite side.

Overall, do the drills you like best and that help you the most, depending on your needs and your stage of advancement. Don't overdo any particular drill.

Keep yourself interested by making your drills as interesting as a championship match.

I usually keep statistics for the drills I do, logging the percentage of successful shots. Or I design a scoring system for the drills where we hit back and forth. This keeps the player interested and trying his best.

17

Return of Serve and Singles Strategy

There are two distinct returns of serve. One is the response to a forceful serve—you block the ball to get it back in your opponent's court. The second is the reply to an easier serve. You drive the ball with pace and with a definite idea of playing it down the line, cross-court, or forcefully down the middle.

For the blocked return, get your racket on the ball with a short and firm action, the racket angle depending on the placement you want. Get the ball over the net without much forward movement of your arm, using the momentum of the incoming ball to get good speed on your return ball.

You need to tighten your grip prior to the impact with the ball and to be very conscious of the angle of your racket, because it will determine both the placement of your shot and whether the ball goes over the net. On this shot the racket face angle should be slightly open, but of course it will vary with each return. The stroke resembles a volley, except that you hit from the ball forward, getting more of a follow-through.

Professional players make sure they get the return of serve in the court. If they get a chance at driving the return they will definitely do it, but their uppermost goal is to get the ball in the court.

They put a lot of pressure on the opponent that way. Balls constantly coming back to the server are a lot more work, and he starts to get the feeling that he has to force the action to finish the point.

That kind of pressure makes for more errors, although a player with a forceful serve has the upper hand. He will get some points on "aces," outright service winners in which the ball gets by his opponent before he can touch it. He will also force his opponent to mis-time and mis-hit service returns, getting more outright service winners.

Those points, added to the normal percentage of return errors, and also some weak returns of serve where it is easy to put the ball away, give the player with a very good first serve a tremendous advantage.

On grass courts, it is unusual to see a good serve-and-volley player lose his service game. The low and uneven bounce of the ball, especially when the grass is damp and slippery, makes returns and passing shots very difficult.

On hard courts there is a great variety in court speeds. It varies according to the roughness and the type of paint coating of the court, and whether it has a cement or asphalt base. If the court is hard, smooth or slick, the game is very fast and that favors the big server.

Some years ago in the U.S. the tendency was to build very fast hard courts, especially for the major championships, favoring the big serve-and-volley players.

Today most hard courts have surfaces that slow down play to where you can play successfully from the backcourt against a net rusher, although a big serve-and-volley player still has an advantage in his service games.

On clay courts you have plenty of time to hit good returns of serve. Just stand behind the baseline to return a hard first serve, using your normal strokes. If your opponent misses the first serve, move inside the baseline to return his second serve. The second serve will most likely be slower or else there is the risk of serving a double fault.

Returning a Twist Serve

Professionals rely on a twist second serve because of its accuracy and safety. They spin the ball so much that, even while clearing the net by two or three feet, the ball still curves down into the service court and then takes a jump.

To return a twist serve successfully you have two choices. The easier one is to move back to let the ball lose some of its height and spin and then drive it back with topspin. The other choice is to move forward to hit the ball before it goes up above your shoulders. This second choice is risky because the ball has not lost its sting, but a firmly blocked return should get the ball in your opponent's court.

Attacking a kick serve after the bounce is a specialty of some top players like McEnroe. It requires perfect timing and a closed racket angle to keep the ball from coming off the racket higher than intended, or off to either side.

Other pros resort to hitting the ball harder than it came into their racket, therefore canceling the effect of these spins. If there is any difficulty on a particular shot they switch to a firmly blocked return.

If you are facing a twist player it takes several service returns to understand what you have to do to block the ball with precision. Don't despair. Even the pros sometimes experience this at the beginning of a match, then they adjust as the match progresses.

Many players have trouble adjusting to a left-handed player's serve because the ball curves and kicks differently. If you are right-handed and a left-hander is curving the ball to your backhand side, you need to move in diagonally to make a dent with your return. Otherwise, the ball will slip farther and farther away. The best option, prior to a tournament match, is to get a player with a similar serve to practice with.

Return of Serve Summary

Get your return of serve in the court, any way you can. Then you can really start the point.

"Finding" the ball is a *must*. Most people think of their stroke first. Against a big serve, they are trained to react right away with the arm. On the contrary, avoid rushing your arm. Get your body as a whole to react first, with your hand and racket finding the ball, then hit.

You need to react fast to a hard serve, but be totally aware of meeting the ball in the center of your racket strings. You need to observe where the ball is going after the bounce in your service court, even if there seems to be no time, or you'll miss more returns than you get in.

As you find the ball, refine your racket angle to control your shot. There isn't much time when receiving a hard serve. But instincts, honed with practice, will help you only if you don't overreact.

Get the ball safely over the net first, then, as you get more accuracy and experience, you can go for better angles and harder returns.

Singles Strategy

Rally game philosophy is very good even when playing a standard match at club level. Of course, you don't hit toward your opponent but slightly away from him to make him sweat it out. Hit to the open court when you have a sure shot. Keep the ball in play, without making silly errors, and you'll slowly learn to win points.

You would be surprised how many people—perhaps ninety percent of the fifty million or so who play tennis—cannot hit as many as twenty balls firmly back and forth in the court.

In club play more points are lost on mistakes or unforced errors than are won by hitting winners. If you keep the ball in play you'll end up winning much more than you lose.

Rallying is the part to learn first. In a match on any medium to slow court, the professionals get into a rally before they start going for winners. You should do the same. Hit several feet over the net with power and plenty of topspin, not only to be safe, but also to get depth and a higher bounce. This will force your opponent to return from farther back, reducing his chances of hitting a winner or a quick shot that can catch you unprepared.

Margin for Error

If your opponent has a weak backhand, or his forehand is a much bigger weapon than his backhand, direct your shots to his backhand side. If your opponent's game is balanced, hit most of your shots crosscourt or down the middle, over the lower part of the net. Avoid making errors or opening up your court. Then, when you start sensing where he's vulnerable, hit the ball there, always keeping a good margin for error. For example, if you know that in the down-the-line drill you need to aim three feet inside the sideline to avoid hitting out, in a match, aim the ball at least three feet inside.

The same goes for height over the net. If aiming one foot over the net results in errors during practice, hit the ball at least two feet over the net, with plenty of topspin, during a match.

Depth

If the ball is bouncing too short in your opponent's court, hit it higher. You'll get more depth and more jump on your shot. It is far less dangerous to hit the ball closer to the service line than to go for the baseline. And it doesn't make sense to hit the ball long when you have enough topspin to make it land well inside the court and make it jump.

Attacking Short Balls

After you hit a forceful shot, move a few steps into your court. Your opponent will likely respond with a shorter or easier shot. As you go forward to get to a shorter ball, hit your groundstrokes lower and with more topspin.

Closing the racket face and pulling up more on the stroke will accomplish that, while still clearing the net. Lower clearance and more topspin is needed because the ball has a shorter trajectory to go down into your opponent's court.

The same goes for passing shots, in which you want the ball to get plenty of topspin so it will dip down soon after crossing the net, making it more difficult for your opponent to volley.

Drifting Back to the Center

When you hit a good crosscourt shot from the backcourt and your opponent is also back, drift slowly toward the middle. It is very likely that your opponent will hit crosscourt, the best percentage shot. You don't want to get caught running fast toward the center of the court while your opponent hits to the place you just left.

If your opponent happens to go down the line with a shot, close to the sideline, he'll be risking much more. In any case you'll be facing slightly in that direction while going slowly toward the middle, so you'll just need to accelerate to get to the ball. Otherwise, if your opponent hits behind you, pivot, and you should be pretty close to the path of the ball.

Hitting Crosscourt

When you are pulled wide, which occurs mostly when receiving a crosscourt shot, hit the ball back crosscourt, so that you don't open the court much to your opponent. A weak shot, of course, would be a setup for him. It will be short and allow him to attack you on either side, to come to the net, etc. But if you hit the ball past your opponent's service line, with plenty of topspin, he won't be able to do much with it.

If you don't have a strong crosscourt shot but are pulled wide, lift the ball high, down the line, but well inside. You could also hit it down the middle, again high and past your opponent's service line. Either choice will give you plenty of time to get back to the middle of your court, ready for the other player's next shot.

At a high level of play, a crosscourt shot would take precedence over any other shot as a return of a good crosscourt shot, unless the opponent has stayed too close to the side he made the shot from, therefore leaving the other side wide open for your down-the-line shot.

The second-best choice would be a high topspin shot, deep down the middle. This is especially true on clay courts. You see the top pros get into crosscourt rallies mixed with down-the-middle shots, risking nothing, waiting for a weaker shot that opens the play for something different.

To show you how dangerous down-the-line shots can be when you are pulled wide, imagine yourself playing someone good, you hit only down the line while the other player hits only good crosscourts. You would soon be out of breath because you are running many more yards to get to each shot than your opponent is.

A good crosscourt shot will pull you beyond your sideline. From there your down-the-line shot cannot be parallel to the sideline, or else it will land outside your opponent's court. You have to angle it toward his court. After the bounce the ball will continue to get closer to the middle, giving him a good chance to cross it the other way where you left a wide open court. Now you have to race all the way across your court. A few shots like that, and you'll feel that you are chasing a rabbit, while your opponent is easily strolling around the court. You may also start to hit short, allowing your opponent to come to the net.

Studying Your Opponent

You need to adjust your game tactics to your opponent's play. Stay cool and see what gives him trouble, what he likes and what throws him off. Unless you know your opponent well, "feel" your opponent at the beginning of a match. Throw some *junk* at him, mixed with your good shots. Many players don't handle a change of pace well, others thrive on your hard shots, making you feel that the better you are playing, the better they play.

Throw some high topspin shots that bounce deep and high, and see how your opponent reacts. If he has trouble, keep it up. It is part of the game. If you are playing competitively, you are not there to hand the match to your opponent, but to beat him or at least to have him sweat it out until the last point is over.

Practice Matches

Practice matches or social matches are different. You try to get the best workout possible. Sometimes your friend across the net doesn't have a good backhand. If you hit mostly to his forehand, you'll get the best possible practice, only reverting to winning tactics if you need to.

In practice focus on consistency and accuracy, rather than raw power. You can hit hard, but use a lot of topspin. The tendency in tournament matches is to hit forward, flattening out the stroke. Practice the other way around, getting your muscles used to lifting the ball. It will be easier to resort to topspin in tight spots in match play.

Rushing the Net

When you approach the net, whether with your forehand or your backhand, a down-the-line approach will cut the angle of your opponent's passing shot. After you hit the ball, continue to advance and stay to the side you made the approach from, perhaps two or three feet from the center line, depending on your shot's depth and how close you get to the net. Your opponent will have only a small opening to pass you with a sharp and short crosscourt, as shown in the following diagrams (player A is yourself and B your opponent):

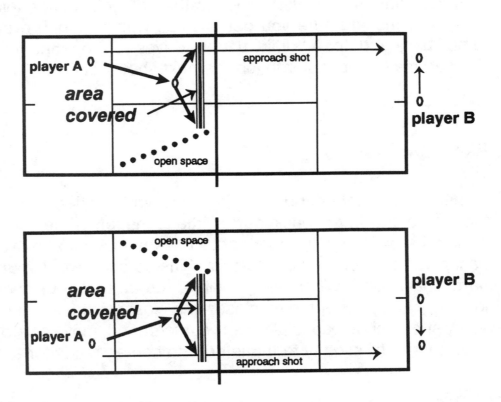

For the average player such a sharp angle is a low percentage shot. Unless he has plenty of topspin, he'll have to resort to hitting a

slow shot to place the ball in the open space, giving you a chance to run it down.

Defending Against a Net Rusher

If you are in your backcourt, and your opponent has made a good approach that doesn't give you much angle to pass him, you can "dink" the ball. You hit it so low and so slow or with so much topspin that the ball goes down to his feet or to his side. From there your opponent will have trouble volleying with pace and usually gives you a shorter ball and a better chance to pass him with your next shot.

If your opponent is very close to the net, your best choice is a good lob, making sure you get the ball well over him even if he jumps back and up. A "dink" usually drives your opponent close to the net, making it easier to lob the next shot over him.

Backcourt Tactics

Let's say a right-hander is playing a right-hander. A very good tactic is to stay in the backcourt a little to the left of the center, and pound the ball into your opponent's backhand, over and over, your backhand crosscourt, your forehand inside out toward your opponent's backhand. Whenever possible, run around your backhand, forcing your opponent to hit closer and closer to the sideline. After every strong shot, especially with your forehand, move a yard inside your court, still slightly to the left of the center, ready for a weaker return.

After a while your opponent will feel pressured. There's not much room for a crosscourt backhand, and he'll risk sending the ball down the line. If he makes a good shot, run it down and hit it with plenty of topspin, high and safely, toward the middle of his backhand side. Then move into the court again, toward the left, and keep pounding his backhand side. As soon as he makes a weaker shot, jump on it crosscourt with your forehand, with plenty of topspin and hard. It should be a safe shot if you get enough topspin, and your opponent will have a hard time reaching it and even more difficulty handling it. If by then you are at the net, you probably have a big open court for your volley, and an easy put-away, or a smash.

This type game requires a lot of patience and very good stamina. Some pros with a big forehand, like Lendl and Agassi, sometimes play two yards to the left of the center of the court, hitting patiently to their opponent's backhand side, pounding their forehands there, or hitting sharp crosscourts when the ball comes to their backhand. They wait for the short ball that they can attack savagely, forcefully, and hit far from their opponent's reach.

When they get to the net the point is already almost won. Unless their opponent, risking everything, hits a miraculous winner or an incredible angle shot, fate is in the attacking player's hands. He has a wide open court to hit either his volley or his smash.

First Serve Percentage

Getting your first serve in is a very good way to put more pressure on your opponent. Even a slower first serve gets treated with more respect than a second serve of the same speed.

If you miss your first serve consistently, the other player will soon be attacking your second serve and making better returns.

You can do the same if your opponent misses his first serve. Move inside the court and attack his second serve.

Crosscourt Service Returns

The safest return of serve is usually crosscourt, over the lowest part of the net and toward the longest extension of the court.

When an opponent is coming to the net following his serve, pounding the ball crosscourt will give you good results. The ball will dip down sooner than a down-the-line shot and it might very well go by your opponent, or give him difficulty, because of the pace. You don't risk making a mistake as much as with a down-the-line return of serve, closer to the sideline and over the higher part of the net.

Steady Tactics

Of course, you would vary all these tactics depending on the degree of success your opponent has in handling them. You can surprise him with a change here and there, but keep winning tactics steady. Don't change a winning game—but always change a losing one.

Don't vary winning tactics just for the sake of change. It might give your opponent a lift and change the whole match.

The same goes for your basic game. You know your best weapons. If you have the fundamentals of this book down well, your consistency will be very high.

Stick to your topspin and the "finish" of your groundstrokes. They will get the ball in the court, and you won't have to resort to frightful halfway strokes.

Stay in the match as long as possible. Don't rush. Keep the ball in play one time more than your opponent and you'll beat players that look much flashier than you.

Overall, respect your opponent and his shots. Never underestimate anyone. If you can beat someone easily, do so without snubbing them. They'll appreciate your game and your behavior. They will also know that the points or games they won they did on their own, without you handing them anything they didn't earn.

And if one player keeps beating you no matter how well you play or how hard you try, recognize that he or she is better than you are. Keep playing your best and learn from the experience. It is possible to improve every day, to learn something good every day. And we learn something every day, whether we recognize it or not.

A positive experience depends only on *you*.

18

Rackets and Balls

Tennis rackets come in a great variety of shapes, materials, and prices. The latest advancements are the larger sizes and the space-age materials used for their construction. That same variety sometimes makes it difficult to choose a racket to learn the game. In this chapter I will give you some help in this respect, and also an idea of what to expect from the rackets available on the market.

Tennis is a game of "feel," and the best way to play it is with a racket that gives you feel. When you start you are striving to learn control. The power of your shots is secondary. You need to spend some time hitting the ball at slower speeds and into the court before you start going for harder shots.

Also, your arm is not yet built up to the strain of hitting hundreds of balls. Therefore, your racket should have some special characteristics that will help you build up both your stroke and your arm.

First, the racket should be light. For an adult, that would be around a 10- to 12½-ounce weight. Second, it is preferable that it have a large size head because the area of lively response, called the sweet spot, is much larger, and you would have no apparent difference on off-center hits, saving your arm from further strain. For the same reason your racket should be very flexible.

The racket should also have a small grip, fitting comfortably in your hand, perhaps a 4¼- or 4⅜-inch circumference for an adult. This may be contrary to common sales practice and "expert" advice, but smaller grips make the racket feel lighter and easier to handle. Cumbersome grips make rackets harder to handle and strain the arm. The choice should be left to the player, who knows what feels most comfortable and manageable in his hand.

Usually the most flexible and inexpensive rackets are made of extruded aluminum, but the industry is quickly developing good quality rackets made of composite materials that are very afford-able.

The larger racket heads, up to 110 square inches of string area, make play easier. They tend to vibrate slightly, but if you put a rubber grommet on the strings, as shown in the picture below, or some other vibration dampener, it stops the vibration.

On the more expensive side there are many kinds of wide-body rackets made of materials such as graphite, kevlar, ceramic, etc. Some of the new tapered rackets are flexible, light, and very responsive, especially with the larger head. They are a pleasure to play with. There are now so many kinds of rackets on the market that you need to get some good advice. If help is not available, just avoid stiff models, heavy rackets, large grips, and small racket heads.

Strings

The more flexible and responsive the racket, the less you'll need to overpower the ball and the more feel you'll get. String thickness and tension will greatly affect the racket's response. In general, thinner strings are more responsive, and tighter string tension will give you more control.

The most popular strings on the market are synthetic strings. They are not as elastic as natural gut, but they are more durable.

It wasn't until the late 1970s that the larger racket head was developed. These rackets give a good response with nylon strings, while with the previous smaller wooden racket models the only high response was obtained when strung with natural gut. Those strings didn't last long but they were the only choice for a world class player.

Today there are many types of synthetic strings available, some of them with incredible response. The best ones require custom stringing and may cost as much as a complete racket at the lower end of the price scale. But they are the choice of the top pros. They may break several sets of strings per match, but they get them free. And they also get paid to advertise them!

You can get the best combination of racket response and control by stringing the racket medium tight with tournament-gauge synthetic gut or fiber. These strings are very thin, seventeen gauge and above, while the normal strings on rackets sold prestrung are usually the thicker sixteen gauge.

Top quality strings make the mid-size racket very responsive. Most professionals use rackets closer to ninety square inches of string area. They feel that the mid-size is the best combination for both power and control. Only the younger crop of professionals are geared toward the larger size. The reason may be that most of the experienced pros in the game today started in their childhood with the smaller racket. The younger professionals, on the other hand, started when the large-size was most popular, possibly prior to the development of the mid-size.

Choosing a Racket

Different combinations of materials such as graphite, fiberglass, boron, and ceramic make the selection of a composite racket very difficult for the beginner or the accomplished player who wants to change to a different racket. Many stores have resorted to lending out "demonstrator" rackets. You can borrow a racket, usually with a sizeable deposit, and try it for a few days.

This is a great service to the player, but the final decision is still not easy. Is this the best racket you can buy? Will the racket respond better with top quality strings? Will it play better at another string tension?

The choice is easier for the beginner. You can start with an inexpensive racket. If you enjoy playing, you may look for a better racket and pass the older one on to someone else.

People who get "hooked" on tennis usually like to get their friends started. Now you know what to do with your older rackets.

You don't need to be a pro to start someone on the right track. This book offers the opportunity for any two beginners or more experienced players to learn the game.

Changing Rackets

Most people aren't too choosy when they select their first racket. But when they already play, they feel that a racket choice may be crucial to their tennis future. And it is, for more reasons than the obvious goal of hitting better shots.

For one, the health and durability of your arm depends on several factors related to your tennis racket: stiffness or flexibility, weight, grip size, and overall size.

At this stage the arm has already developed itself around the racket's characteristics. It has gotten used to the string tension, the racket weight, the grip size, as well as the racket's flexibility and response.

The player's technique and detailed muscle work has been conditioned instinctively from experience with his first racket. Going to another racket may be a traumatic experience. Mis-hits with a stiffer racket, or one with a smaller sweet spot, go right down the arm.

It is a delicate proposition, to say the least. You either build up your muscles and your technique gradually for the greater demands of a stiffer, heavier racket, or you end up on the long list of players with "tennis elbow," or some other physical problem.

On the brighter side, if your technique is very good and you have the patience to start slowly and deliberately, drilling one shot at a time, your muscles may respond well.

Here is my advice:

1) To start learning, choose a very flexible light racket or get one with very responsive strings.

2) Be very selective when you change racket brands or models. Of course, you can upgrade your equipment, like the top stars. But keep in mind that they get customized equipment, a contract, and usually so much practice time that the new racket gets to feel like a part of their body, just like the old one did.

3) Make the stress factor on your arm your most important consideration. You'll have to try the new racket and trust your feel, watching for signs of pain or stress. One of the most dangerous signals is pain appearing in any joint, such as your wrist, elbow, or shoulder. The tendons attach the musculature to these joints, and they are harder to repair than the muscles themselves. The rest period necessary to fully repair a tendon can feel "infinitely" long.

Shorter Rackets

Shorter rackets, much lighter and with a large head, are excellent for children. There are plenty of these on the market. The best type is very flexible, light, with a large head, a short throat and a small handle that fits comfortably in a child's hand. With these I have been able to teach children as young as four and five years old.

When those were not available I cut two to six inches off old adult rackets and used them not only for children but to teach adults as well. Shorter rackets are a very successful teaching tool. The tennis industry would do well to develop shorter learning rackets for adults, similar to the Graduated Length Method used in teaching snow skiing.

For the beginner, the shorter racket makes finding, feeling and controlling the ball much easier. Students go for control rather than power and they enjoy hitting back and forth at the slower ball speed. With the techniques shown in this book, it makes tennis a very easy sport to learn.

Students learn quicker with a shorter racket. Next I have them use a normal size racket, while "choking" up on the handle, as explained in Chapter Seven. From there, they move the hand gradually to a normal grip position. But these adjustments are different from individual to individual, depending on their feel and confidence.

Tennis Balls

In the U.S. tennis balls are very lively, while in some other countries the balls have some characteristics that make them slower or harder to propel.

Some European balls, for example, come in boxes, while in the U.S. they are packed in pressurized cans. Professional players resort to lowering the string tension while playing with the slower European ball to get more ball speed and feel.

There are two distinct types of balls: one is for clay courts, the other for hard courts. The advertised difference is that the hard court balls last much longer on hard courts, which is basically true. The same can't be said for the player's arm. The hard court balls are somewhat stiffer, less flexible, less lively.

The regular balls, or clay court balls, are softer, have a much better feel and cause a lot less stress on the arm, to the point that many professional tournaments played on hard courts have chosen the regular ball over the hard court ball.

Personally, I always coach with the regular ball, whether on hard courts or clay courts, saving my students' arms and my own. The only exception would be in preparing someone to play a tournament in which other balls were used. In this case it is best to choose the exact brand and type so that the player adjusts to the conditions he'll have to face later on.

Hard courts can also stress your arm. A beginning tennis player doesn't hit consistently in the center of the string area. When the less-responsive area of the strings comes into play, the stress of the impact is greater on the arm. This situation is compounded with a faster ball. Hard court surfaces don't slow the ball much. A fast ball will continue traveling with quite some speed. If you mis-hit it, you'll feel it on your arm.

Avoid stressing your arm until you have built it up to the task. As a beginner, have your partner play or toss the ball deliberately slow.

Good technique will help your arm immensely, as well as concentrating on finding the ball really well.

19

Tennis Courts

There are four major types of court:

1 Clay courts, either American green Har-Tru™ or Fast-Dry™, or European-type red clay. Clay courts are soft, gentle on your feet and legs, and absorb part of the impact of the ball on the ground, slowing it down.

2) Hard courts, made of a cement or asphalt base and an acrylic surface coating. Hard courts are quite fast. To slow down the court the surface is usually roughed up by mixing the coating with sand or rubber granules. The more granules in the mix, the slower the court will play.

3) Grass courts, made of special grass, cut very short, similar to golf greens.

4) Carpets of many kinds and materials, usually used indoors.

Lines on clay courts are usually plastic tapes nailed down to the ground. Lines on hard courts are painted on the surface, and lines on grass courts are laid down with chalk or special paint.

If you have the chance to learn on clay, do so. The soft surface is easier on your legs. Your feet don't stick as they do on hard courts. Turns and pivots on clay courts are harmless and natural. Another advantage is that the bounce of the ball on the softer surface slows it down considerably, giving you extra time before the swing. Practicing on clay for a considerable amount of time reinforces the habit of reading the second curve of the ball, the one after the bounce, and adjusting to it.

On hard court surfaces, players usually do not learn at very slow speeds. From rushing and hitting hard, they get the feeling that there is no time, that they have to start swinging prior to the bounce of the ball. It is a faulty mental computation that may stay with the player for the rest of his life and interfere with the improvement of his groundstrokes.

If you always play on fast courts, you may not know the difference. But if you get to a tournament level and play on all surfaces, you'll know.

I recall many U.S. junior champions, particularly from California, where most courts are of cement or asphalt base, playing on clay courts at the Orange Bowl in Miami, the largest international junior tournament in the world. They didn't make it past the early rounds in singles. Players dominant in their age categories were utter failures on clay. They had extraordinary serve-and-volley games, but their hard-court-developed groundstrokes were not up to the task.

A Bit of History

Back through the '60s and '70s many top American players avoided the early part of the European tournament season, played on red clay, and went directly to England just prior to Wimbledon to play on grass. From there they came back to America to play several grass court tournaments in preparation for the grass courts of Forest Hills (now the U.S. Open). After that it was California and hard courts, then to Australia for the grass court tour.

Except for some great champions who were good on any surface, like Chuck McKinley, Jimmy Connors, John McEnroe, Vitas Gerulaitis, and some clay court specialists, like Cliff Richey from Texas, and Florida's Frank Froehling, Harold Solomon, and Eddie Dibbs, most Americans had weaknesses on the slower clay. From Tony Trabert in 1955, to Michael Chang in 1989, it took 34 years for an American male to win again on the red clay of the French Open.

The American viewpoint of the Davis Cup was almost the same story. The clay courts were to be avoided. The "Challenge Round" rule was in effect—the champion nation sat comfortably at home, waiting for the elimination rounds to determine their final challenger. The sole survivor had to play, of course, on the Cup Holder's grounds, which were usually the grass courts of Australia and the U.S. To compound this situation, the interzone finals were played in the Cup Holder's country and usually on grass.

From the end of World War II in 1945, when the Davis Cup was resumed, until 1960, the U.S. and Australia played every single Challenge Round.

Wresting the Davis Cup from those two giants was nearly impossible. They had legions of players over the years who were masters of the serve-and-volley game, and the Davis Cup was safely tucked away.

A Different Viewpoint

Two interesting developments occurred in the 1960s, increasing the challenges to Australia and the U.S. The interzone final went to the home-and-away rule for the first time. The U.S. lost on red clay to Italy in Rome in 1961, to Mexico in Mexico City (Zone match) in 1962, and regained the Cup in 1963 in Australia on grass. At home in 1964 for the Challenge Round, the U.S. chose to play on clay and lost to Australia, then again lost on clay to Spain in Barcelona in 1965.

To simplify matters for America in the American Zone, up to that time there was a simple rule that said that the finals between the North American Zone and the South American Zone had to be played "within the confines of the North American Zone." In the International Lawn Tennis Federation meeting in London in 1965 yours truly made the motion that this rule should be changed and replaced with the home-and-away concept. The U.S. had to go to the slow courts of South America, with some painful losses. But the presence of the U.S. team in those countries, coupled with the intense competition and the sellout crowds, spearheaded an incredible development of tennis in South America, which had been precisely the argument I put forward favoring the rule change.

The abolition of the Challenge Round system in 1972 was another blow to Australia and the U.S. Now the Cup Holder had to go through the elimination rounds the same as anyone else. The Davis Cup was finally equally open to any country, and the best teams visited many countries around the world. This made tennis grow worldwide with great intensity, a phenomenon that hasn't stopped since.

I know that American players must sometimes feel like guinea pigs when confronted with difficult conditions and unfavorable crowds in other countries, but these players' participation is perhaps their greatest contribution to keeping the game truly international.

Hard Courts Versus Clay Courts

Aided by clay as their main surface, countries like Spain, Rumania, Sweden, Czechoslovakia, Germany, Italy, Argentina, and many others developed legions of youngsters with superb groundstrokes. Many of them made it to the top ranks.

Chris Evert of Fort Lauderdale, Florida, and John McEnroe at the Port Washington Tennis Academy in Long Island, New York, were no exceptions to this rule, practicing and playing many junior tournaments on clay.

The U.S. made an excursion into using clay courts for their top tournament at Forest Hills. The stadium grass courts could not stand the wear and tear of the two-week U.S. Open Championships. Many players criticized the courts. Finally, in 1975, the grass court surface was replaced with Har-Tru™, an American clay with superb characteristics including reduced physical stress on the legs, excellent drainage that allows play even in light rain, and faster speed of play than European clay courts.

European clay courts can be exhausting for a player because they are very slow and points are so hard fought that it is not unusual to see a ball going back and forth fifty times or more in just one point. The Har-Tru™ surface, on the other hand, can be made faster or slower by merely changing the amount of rolling done to the court, adding or scraping off loose material, as well as regulating the watering of the court.

The Har-Tru™ clay court surface was kept for three years. Chris Evert was invincible, winning all three championships played on clay. She actually had a clay court winning streak of 125 matches, all the way from 1973 to 1979.

On the men's side there were many interesting matches, and Jimmy Connors made it to all three finals, winning in 1976, in perhaps his finest victory, over Bjorn Borg.

But the U.S. Open, in the wake of a huge tennis boom, needed a larger, better site, and, unlike the West Side Tennis Club at Forest Hills, one totally under the control of the United States Tennis Association.

Perhaps because of the threat of domination of the softer surfaces by the foreign clay court specialists—such as Bjorn Borg, Guillermo Vilas, Manuel Orantes, and many young overseas players—U.S. officials went to their hard court formula. They built the new home for the U.S. Open at the Flushing Meadows site of the old Louis Armstrong stadium, near La Guardia airport, in 1978.

The hard courts of that time were quite fast, and many times were painted lengthwise to make them smoother and even faster. West Coast tournaments and Davis Cup matches had shown practically no rallies, and the spectacle was as good as an Old West shoot-out. It was a far cry from the beautiful artistry we had seen on clay at Forest Hills and in the European events, including Wimbledon's center court, where the grass was very short, slowing down play which allowed some success from the backcourt, too.

Over the years, under pressure from players and the media, hard courts at the U.S. Open and other major tournaments have been slowed down. Players can now play successfully from the back-court. But in order to slow down hard courts the surface is made either coarser or softer, mixing sand with the coating or using rubber-like components. The resistance to turning your feet is greater than in any other court surface, with much higher stress on ankles, knees, and hips.

For top flight tennis players, who fight each point and each match no matter how long, this type of hard court is the most taxing in the world. Careers have been cut short due to leg and lower back injuries, while players who played mostly on clay and grass have generally had much longer careers.

A partial solution to cut down on knee injury on slow hard courts is to use smooth sole tennis shoes, except when the surface is slip-pery. The smooth shoe sole makes it easier to turn, diminishing the stress factor on the legs.

The Hard Court Boom

From 1975 to 1977, when the U.S. Open was played on clay courts, the major tournaments leading to Forest Hills were now on clay to foster top players' participation. The most important part of the American tour was on clay. This started a boom of Har-Tru™ and Fast-Dry™ clay court construction in the U.S., except on the West Coast. More than 5,000 of those courts were built.

But in 1978 the U.S. Open changed to hard courts and many other American tournaments also switched. Practically all the major professional tournaments in the U.S. were either on indoor carpets or hard courts.

Following this wake, still in the midst of the incredible tennis boom of the '70s, tens of thousands of hard courts were built in schools, clubs, and private homes. The U.S. Open had set the trend.

Today, the main surface for a youngster in America is fast hard courts.

And America is paying the price. Hard courts, together with the conventional teaching techniques prevalent in the U.S., have made flat hitting from the backcourt the rule. Heavy topspin is the exception of a privileged few, like Courier, Krickstein, Agassi and Chang.

U.S. players do very well around U.S. Open time, when the competition is on hard courts. But overall, with over twenty million tennis players, the U.S. is not in the commanding international position it could be. Countries with a fraction of that number of players are head and shoulders above America. From 1985 to 1991, U.S.-born male and female players have captured five Grand Slam titles, vs. Czechoslovakia's seventeen, West Germany's fifteen and Sweden's nine. Since its 1984 final round Davis Cup loss to Sweden, the U.S. did not again reach the finals until 1990, when the aforementioned young topspin players came to the rescue and won it in the U.S.—on red clay.

It is not by accident that most of the world's best tennis pros in the last fifteen years are players with plenty of experience and practice on clay courts in their younger years, including Evert and McEnroe.

The most successful and famous tennis academies and training centers in the world have clay courts. Clay is a surface that helps develop key features of the backcourt strokes and the backcourt game. Hard courts, on the other hand, help develop volleys and court sense at the net.

Ideally, a player should first develop groundstrokes, then the net game. Again, if you start on hard courts and want to be good, begin at slow speeds and develop your topspin groundstrokes. Next work on the backhand slice and on your serve. Then concentrate on your net game until you volley like a pro.

Tennis associations, clubs, cities, schools and colleges must make slow courts available to developing youth. If they are clay courts, better still.

California, almost 100 percent hard courts, would do well in changing the trend.

Prophecy? Perhaps.

20

General Rules and Competition

Tennis is governed by an international set of rules laid down by the International Tennis Federation and adopted by the United States Tennis Association.

Called Rules of Tennis and Cases and Decisions, these rules, together with The Code, cover every aspect of the game of tennis, from size and make of courts, tennis balls and rackets, to scoring, competition, and correct behavior.

The Rules of Tennis and Cases and Decisions have been extended with U.S.T.A. comments that clarify them to a far-reaching extent. Complete copies of these Rules and The Code can be purchased from the U.S.T.A., 707 Alexander Road, Princeton, New Jersey 08540.

Some of these rules have been covered in earlier chapters in a simplified manner. This chapter deals with additional general aspects of the rules.

The server shall not serve until the receiver is ready, whether it is a first or a second serve. If the receiver attempts to return the serve, he shall be deemed ready. Otherwise, should he indicate that he wasn't ready, a "let" will be played, repeating the same serve.

A "let" can be called for a hindrance in making a shot, outside the player's control, but not the result of a permanent fixture of the court. For example, if a ball from an adjacent court comes into your court while the ball is in play, a "let" is called and the whole point is replayed, with the server getting a first serve.

A player may toss the ball up to serve, then decide to catch the ball instead, directly or after bouncing on the ground. Unless he attempted to strike it, he can replay the serve.

Any ball touched by a player before it lands outside his court is deemed to have landed in. Many players catch the ball outside the court during friendly competition, calling it out, but in any argument, remember that the rule states that if it touches you before landing, it is good.

A ball touching a line is deemed to have landed in the court of which that line is boundary. Any ball that you cannot call out with certainty should be regarded as good.

The Code determines further rulings on decisions not covered by the Rules of Tennis and Cases and Decisions. For example:

In the event a match is played without officials, each player calls the balls on his side, but should be scrupulously honest and fair to his opponent. If he can't call it out, there is no maybe. It is good.

The calls should also be instantaneous. If you called it incorrectly and the ball you called out is good, you've lost the point.

The server should announce the score in points prior to serving each point. (This is a tradition kept by good players since the beginning of time.)

Obscenities and bad language are considered "unsportsmanlike" conduct, as well as abusing the ball or tennis equipment. In officiated matches such infractions are penalized.

Making loud noises can be the basis for a "let" or a hindrance, and should be avoided.

If you become a serious player, ready to compete, realize that there are innumerable situations not covered here that you may need to resolve quickly. Knowing the answer in advance is the best solution to avoiding problems in your matches that can result in an impaired performance. Copies of both publications can be obtained from the U.S.T.A. Publications Department.

Competition

The U.S.T.A. is an exceedingly well-managed organization, dedicated to controlling, promoting, and developing all aspects of the game in the U.S.

The U.S.T.A. has approximately 435,000 members distributed over seventeen Sectional Tennis Associations, some of which comprise several states. Each section is a separate tennis organization, divided into districts, each with its own representatives and affiliated tennis facilities.

As an example, one of the U.S.T.A. sections, the Florida Tennis Association (F.T.A.), has close to 500 affiliated tennis facilities in its sixteen districts. The F.T.A. has a year-long calendar of tournaments in all age categories, plus major tournaments involving top professionals as well, including the Lipton International in Miami, which brings almost every pro in the game to Florida. Altogether, over 600 sanctioned tournaments are played in Florida each year.

Age categories in tournaments are 10 and under, 12, 14, 16, and 18 for boys and girls. For adults, the categories are Open Division, 25 and over, 30, 35, 40, 45, 50, 55, 60, 65, 70, 75, 80, and 85. There are also some special doubles divisions, like husband and wife, father and daughter, father and son, mother and daughter, mother and son, brother and brother, brother and sister, etc.

Several tournaments, including the U.S.T.A. League and the new 50-and-Over League, use a special rating system, the NTRP (National Tennis Rating Program) to classify and separate players according to their level. The U.S.T.A. Leagues are team competitions and have regional, sectional, and national playoffs.

Senior tennis is extremely popular, not only at the local, state and national level, but around the world as well. There are international tournaments in age categories above 35, 45, 50, and older. The U.S.T.A. is increasingly associating some of this competition with the most serious tournaments. Where years ago pro players were washed up, competitively speaking, in their early thirties, today you see former world champions in their forties and fifties playing for prize money in front of enthusiastic crowds.

Each section publishes its own yearbook, in which every affiliated tennis facility is listed, with address and phone number if available, a complete schedule of tournaments, leagues, rankings, offices, and officials to contact, and a host of services such as recreational tennis programs, U.S.T.A. school programs, teacher training workshops, programs for the disabled, video and film library, and many more.

The following list shows where you can order your section's yearbook.

U.S.T.A. SECTIONS

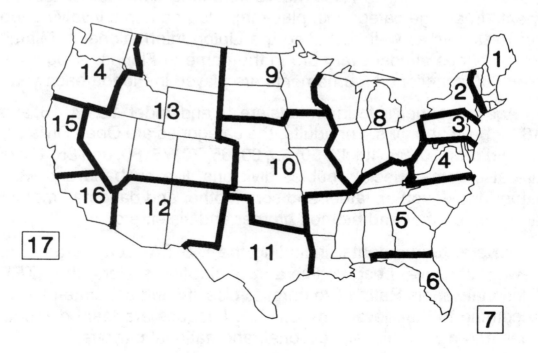

1. New England Tennis Association: (617) 964-2030
2. Eastern Tennis Association: (914) 698-0414
3. Middle States Tennis Association: (215) 768-4040
4. Mid-Atlantic Tennis Association: (703) 560-9480
5. Southern Tennis Association: (404) 257-1297
6. Florida Tennis Association: (305) 652-2866
7. Caribbean Tennis Association (includes Puerto Rico and the U.S. Virgin Islands): (809) 765-3182
8. Western Tennis Association: (317) 577-5130
9. Northwestern Tennis Association: (612) 546-0709
10. Missouri Valley Tennis Association: (816) 556-0777
11. Texas Tennis Association: (512) 443-1334
12. Southwestern Tennis Association : (602) 921-8964
13. Intermountain Tennis Association: (303) 695-4117
14. Pacific Northwest Tennis Association (includes Alaska and British Columbia): (503) 245-3048
15. Northern California Tennis Association: (415) 748-7373
16. Southern California Tennis Association: (213) 208-3838
17. Hawaii Pacific Tennis Association (includes Guam and Samoa): (808) 955-6696

Another publication you might want is the U.S.T.A Tennis Yearbook. This is a marvelous documentation of the incredibly complex but organized role of the U.S.T.A. in the tennis game, as well as a historical record of major championships and events. It also lists all its offices, officers, committees, representatives, rankings, champions, the season's results (both professional and amateur), awards, prize money, sketches of the top U.S. players, official rules of tennis, constitution and bylaws of the U.S.T.A., tournament regulations, and much more.

The U.S.T.A. has several player development programs. A typical "roots" program is the U.S.T.A./National Junior Tennis League, designed to bring tennis to those eight to eighteen years old. It has 280 chapters spread throughout the U.S., with an enrollment above 100,000, from novice to intermediate levels.

The U.S.T.A. Tennis Yearbook can be ordered from the U.S.T.A. at the address shown on page 247. The U.S.T.A. phone number is (609) 452-2580.

A Game for Life

Tennis is a sport for the being, rather than the mind. The being thrives on feeling, on aesthetics, on beautiful coordinated moves, while the mind thrives on pictures, perfect poses, right-wrong computations.

The best tennis pros are artists who operate at the higher harmonics of aesthetic flows, with little thought involved, just like concert pianists at their best.

Life seems full of pressures. But we can all be artists, provided we deal with those pressures which we ourselves created.

Some players misbehave. In tennis, as in life, there is no reason for bad manners. Having good manners, good attitude, grace in winning, and coolness in defeat, doesn't hurt anyone.

Be a master of control. Show it with your emotions and your behavior.

If your opponent acts up you can show dignity, cool disapproval if you like, or you can stay uninvolved. Today's championship rules penalize unsportsmanlike conduct and those rules should always be enforced. Someday everybody will realize that sportsmanship is the best way to survive.

More and more the best players today act like the supreme artists they are. Regardless of the pressure of the media for sensational stories, these pros respect the rules, other players and officials, and don't lose their control.

It wasn't always like that. Credit is due to those who are regulating the sport. Tennis couldn't exist without rules and the contributions from the many officials who regulate and promote the game.

Tennis wouldn't have grown, either, without the legions of "aficionados," the media, tennis teachers, club managers, volunteer committee members, aspiring youngsters, and helpful parents.

To all of you, everyone involved in tennis, my greatest admiration and thanks. Your actions are appreciated in this sport that is moving forward, stellarly, into a brilliant future among all sports.

About the Author

Oscar Wegner is an internationally known professional tennis coach and a former touring player on the international circuit. A dedicated world traveler, he has also served as a teaching pro and tennis director for tennis federations, cities, clubs, academies, schools and camps in several countries.

A native of Buenos Aires, Argentina, Wegner traded his engineering studies for a far more exciting tennis career. From 1963 to 1967 he played the international tennis circuit in the United States, Europe, South America, Africa and the Caribbean. While playing and practicing with many of the top players of the 50s, 60s and 70s, he compared notes with them and began his inquiry into the secrets of their success.

In 1968 Wegner embarked on a coaching career, first as an assistant to Pancho Segura at the famous Beverly Hills Tennis Club in California. It was there that he made the crucial observation that tennis was being taught one way while the pros played a different way.

Wegner set out to resolve this discrepancy. His research led him to isolate the actual basics of tennis that apply to any player at any level, whether a pro or a beginner. He developed, as well, a teaching methodology to communicate those basics to players and coaches alike. This approach, from its inception, has produced remarkable results, not only in Wegner's hands, but by other coaches using his methods.

In 1973 he served as the Junior Davis Cup Captain for Spain and as coach with the National Tennis School. That country was then at a crossroads in terms of which direction its tennis instruction should take. Wegner's views in favor of the modern topspin game prevailed. To this day, topspin strokes remain a major feature of Spain's international success.

Wegner has also held prominent coaching positions in Germany, Brazil and the U.S., where he has coached highly ranked professionals and top international juniors. His students have also included thousands of recreational players, as well as famous athletes and luminaries from the entertainment field.

His results, fully documented and endorsed by top players, teaching pros, tennis directors and officials, make tennis an easy sport to learn at any age. His approach to modern tennis technology has truly closed the gap between the way tennis is conventionally taught and the way top pros play. His methods are revolutionizing the entire field of tennis instruction.

Index